Prehistoric Origami

Dinosaurs and Other Creatures

Other Antroll books by John Montroll:

Origami Sculptures

Prehistoric Origami

Dinosaurs And Other Creatures

Antroll Publishing Company
Vermont

John Montroll

To Carol Ann, Kathleen, Martha, Mark, Jan, and Mark

Library of Congress Catalog Card Number: 88-84160

ISBN 1-877656-01-1

Introduction

My goal with this latest collection of original projects has been to use origami to create an accurate and aesthetically pleasing collection of prehistoric animals. The presentation of animals in this book reflects the most current paleontological theories, from nomenclature (the Apatosaurus has replaced the recently decanonized Brontosaurus from my paper menagerie) to fine structural detail (note, for example, the dorsal plating on the Stegosaurus). I hope that the resulting work provides the reader/user with both a technically accurate survey of these extinct creatures and many hours of artistic pleasure.

Although any square paper can be used for the projects in this book, the best material is origami paper. One type, Zenagraf Papers, has very attractive computer generated designs. Origami paper is sold in many hobby shops, and can be purchased by mail from The Friends of The Origami Center of America, 15 West 77 Street, New York, NY 10024-5192. Large sheets of paper are easier to work with than smaller ones. Origami paper is colored on one side and white on the other. In the diagrams in this book, the shading represents the colored side.

Those readers seasoned in the ways of origami can start to work immediately on the more advanced projects in this book. For novices, I have included a pictorial introduction to folding techniques, one much more extensive than is usually found in a project book of this type. The first few projects are designed to help master origami basics. More elaborate designs follow.

This book is a combination of the old and the modern. The ancient art here is illustrated step-by-step with graphics produced on a computer. The illustration conforms to internationally accepted Randlett-Yoshizawa method, which readers of my earlier books have found very useful. The directions for each project have been submitted to experienced origami artists, and I thank the many friends whose suggestions have helped me improve the clarity of my illustrations and explanations.

Other friends have helped in other ways. Martha Landy has provided an excellent introduction and background notes on the animals. Ms. Landy teaches students with special needs in North Brunswick, New Jersey. Her class has produced "Dinosaur Day" for the past eight years at John Adams Elementary School. Her students research and explain dinosaurs and celebrate them with the entire school. In addition to her personal passion for dinosaurs, Ms. Landy finds them one of the most motivating educational tools.

Rosalind Joyce has made valuable contributions to this book through her research and suggestions on the techniques of wet folding. Her methods enable origami artists to infuse their work with more three-dimensional detail than most of us had thought possible. She folded for us fine specimens of some of the animals in this book. My brother Andy photographed these models for our illustrations. Both he and my brother Mark have assisted me throughout this project. I give thanks to these talented people, without whose help this book could not have been completed.

John Montroll

Contents

Mountain & Volcano
Page 16

Cracked Dinosaur Egg
Page 18

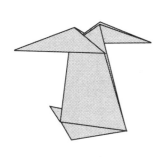

Prehistoric Tree
Page 20

Parasaurolophus
Page 26

Struthiomimus
Page 32

Kuehneosaurus
Page 36

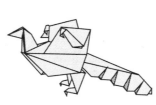

Archaeopteryx
Page 41

Pterodactylus
Page 47

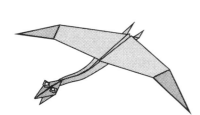

Quetzalcoatlus
Page 53

Rhamphorynchus
Page 59

Pteranodon
Page 65

Elasmosaurus
Page 72

Tanystropheus
Page 76

Apatosaurus
Page 80

Brachiosaurus
Page 86

Dimetrodon
Page 89

Spinosaurus
Page 94

Tyrannosaurus
Page 100

Hadrosaurus
Page 106

Iguanodon
Page 111

Protoceratops
Page 119

Triceratops
Page 124

Stegosaurus
Page 135

PREHISTORIC ORIGAMI

To Define a Dinosaur

Dinosaurs lived in the Mesozoic (mezz-oh-ZOE-ik) Era which began 225 millions years ago and lasted for 155 million years. Mesozoic means "middle life". The era is divided into three periods.

Dinosaurs appeared on Earth during the Triassic (try-ASS-ik) Period. It lasted for 45 million years. All the continents were connected in one giant land mass. There were only a few kinds of dinosaur. These were mostly small, quick, meat eaters.

The Jurassic (joo-RASS-ik) Period began 180 million years ago and lasted for 45 million years. The continents began to move apart and shallow seas and swamps formed. The climate was tropical. The largest dinosaurs lived at this time.

The Cretaceous (kre-TAY-shus) Period is the time the most varieties of dinosaurs lived. It was 65 million years long. The continents were well separated. The climate was seasonal and flowers appeared on earth for the first time.

To be a dinosaur an animal must have a specific skull and hip structure. One way scientists classify reptiles is by the number of holes in the back of the skull. These holes may be to accommodate jaw muscles. They lighten the weight of the skull. All dinosaurs are diapsids (di-AP-sids), having two holes in their skulls.

The Ornithischian (orn-ith-ISK-ee-an) dinosaurs have the two lower bones of the hip pointing towards the back. They have a beak-like addition to the jaw bone. Some were plant eaters and some were meat eaters. Ornithischian means "bird-hipped". The Saurischian (sawr-ISK-ee-an) dinosaurs have each hip bone pointing in a different direction. They have a solid jaw and are meat eaters. Saurischian means "lizard-hipped".

All true dinosaurs were land dwellers. However, some dinosaurs, like many other land dwelling animals, would sometimes wade or swim.

Martha Landy

Wet Folding

Sometime, you find that thick, textured, or leathery papers in your collection look like they would make wonderful origami, until you work with them. After very few folds, they become torn and ugly. If a favorite sheet has become old and brittle, it does not fold well, either; it breaks!

Before you give up on uncooperative paper, try wet folding. The results are greater flexibility and solid, long-lasting models. As the paper dries, its own adhesives hold your folds stiffly and permanently. (Purists ignore this: A drop or two of white GLUE to a cup of water adds body to soft paper.)

How much water should be used? The amount varies with the kind of paper you choose. Start by dampening the underside of your paper with a squeezed out washcloth or sponge. A spray bottle or wet hands work just as well. Soaking the paper makes it fall apart. If it gets too wet, wait until some water evaporates. Wet folding can be messy. Some papers flop apart when you least appreciate it.

Fold your models slowly and carefully, with fingertips, not nails. Sharp creases can tear. While you fold, notice how moisture evaporates from different papers at different rates. Re-wet parts of the model as you work, so that your paper stays flexible.

An added attraction is to make the model three dimensional. While it is still wet, the head, tail, legs, and body can be rolled or pinched to look like hollow, 3-D tubes. Many models will dry as you handle them and mold them into place. If others do not stay in position while you shape them, use paper clips or thin wire to keep them where you want them. The wire can pose each part, like a sculpture, creating the exact personality you prefer for the model. Remove wire and clips after the paper is dry.

Unlike foil that remembers every mistake you made, you can re-wet and re-fold small parts of your model without ruining it. This is helpful when making adjustments for free standing subjects.

Depending on the type of paper, your model will dry within a few minutes to overnight. If you discover that your masterpiece was made from waterproof, vinyl coated paper, just be more patient! From simple folds to the ridiculously complex, wet folding adds another dimension to your origami.

Rosalind Joyce

The Basic Folds

1. Valley Fold.

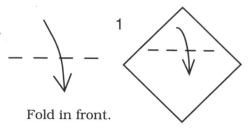

Fold in front.

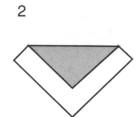

2. Mountain Fold.

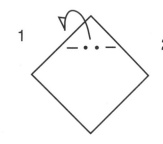

Fold behind.

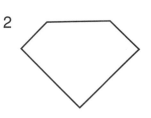

3. Turn over.

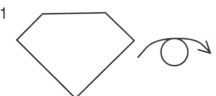

4. Unfold / Pull Out.

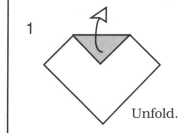

Unfold.

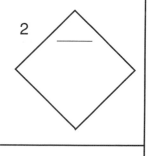

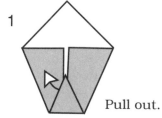

Pull out.

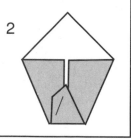

5. Crease Line.

———————

Crease lines represent creases in the paper and are drawn as thin lines which generally do not touch the edges.

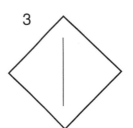

1   2

Unfold.

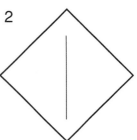

3

What it really looks like.

6. Fold and Unfold.

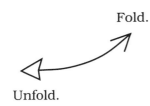

Fold.

Unfold.

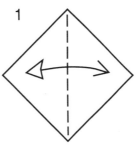

1   2

Fold and unfold.

7. Approximations.

The drawings are usually inaccurate, intended to give more information.

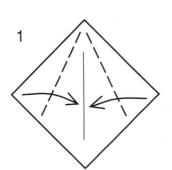

1   2

(This is the kite fold.)

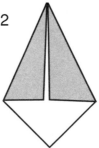

2

What it really looks like.

8. For each step. Always look one step ahead. For example, before folding step 1, look at step 2 also.

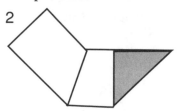

9. Rabbit Ear.

To fold a rabbit ear, one corner is folded in half and laid down to a side.

See steps 1-10 of the Prehistoric Tree (page 20) for a detailed folding method of this rabbit ear.

See steps 2-8 of the Parasaurolophus (page 26) for a detailed folding method of this rabbit ear.

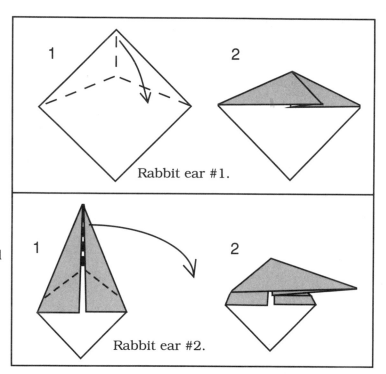

Rabbit ear #1.

Rabbit ear #2.

10. Double Rabbit Ear. If you were to bend a straw you would be doing the double rabbit ear.

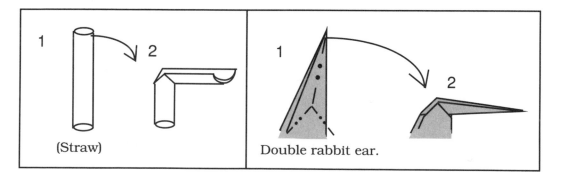

(Straw)

Double rabbit ear.

11. Place Your Finger Here.   Several kinds of folds use this arrow. It is placed between layers of paper and shows where to place your finger to accomplish the fold. Several examples follow.

12. Squash Fold.   In a squash fold, some paper is opened and then made flat. The shaded arrow shows where to place your finger.

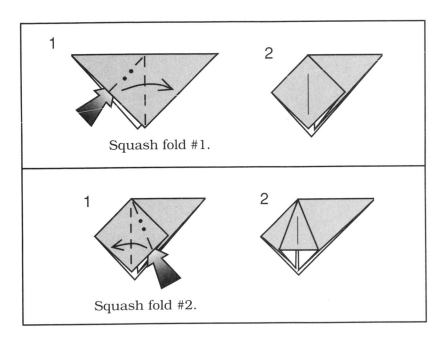

Squash fold #1.

Squash fold #2.

13. Petal Fold.

In a petal fold, one point is folded up while two opposite sides meet each other.

For a detailed explanation of this petal fold, see steps 11-18 of the Bird Base (page 23).

For a detailed explanation of this petal fold, see steps 12-16 of the Frog Base (page 57).

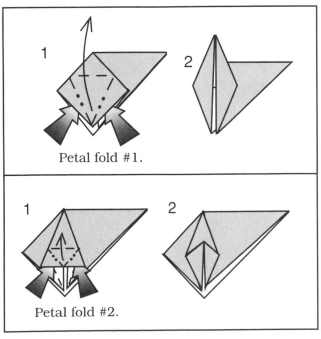

Petal fold #1.

Petal fold #2.

14. Inside Reverse Fold.

Since the inside reverse fold is used more often than the outside reverse fold, it is usually just called a reverse fold. Here are several examples of inside reverse folds.

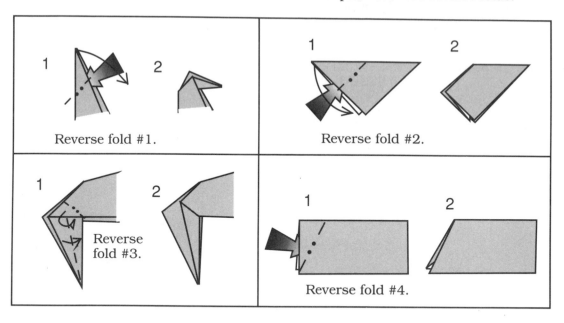

Reverse fold #1.

Reverse fold #2.

Reverse fold #3.

Reverse fold #4.

15. Outside Reverse Fold.

In the process of doing an outside reverse fold, much of the paper must be unfolded.

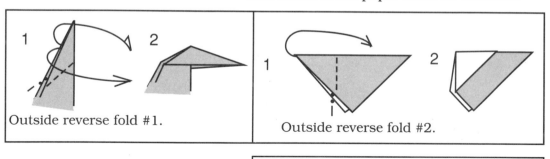

Outside reverse fold #1.

Outside reverse fold #2.

16. Crimp Fold.

A crimp fold is a combination of two reverse folds.

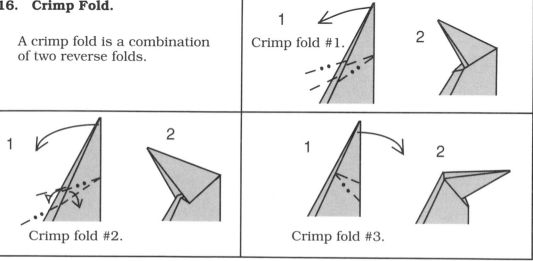

Crimp fold #1.

Crimp fold #2.

Crimp fold #3.

PREHISTORIC ORIGAMI

17. Push In Arrow. This arrow is usually used for sink folds and three dimensional folding.

18. Sink Fold. In a sink fold, some of the paper which contain no edges is folded inside. To do this fold, much of the model must be unfolded.

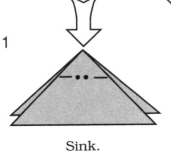

1

2

Sink.

19. Three Dimensional Folding. 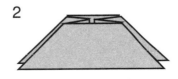 In several animals, the last step is to make them three dimensional by pushing in some paper.

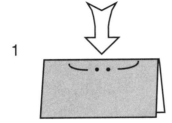

1

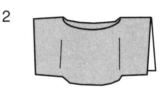

2

20. Spread Squash Fold.

A cross between a squash fold and sink fold, some paper in the center is spread apart and then made flat.

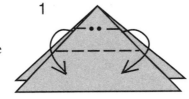

1

2

Spread squash fold.

21. X-ray or Guide Line. -

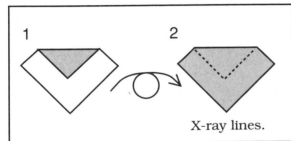

1   2

X-ray lines.

1   2

Fold to the dotted line.

THE BASIC FOLDS   15

Mountain and Volcano

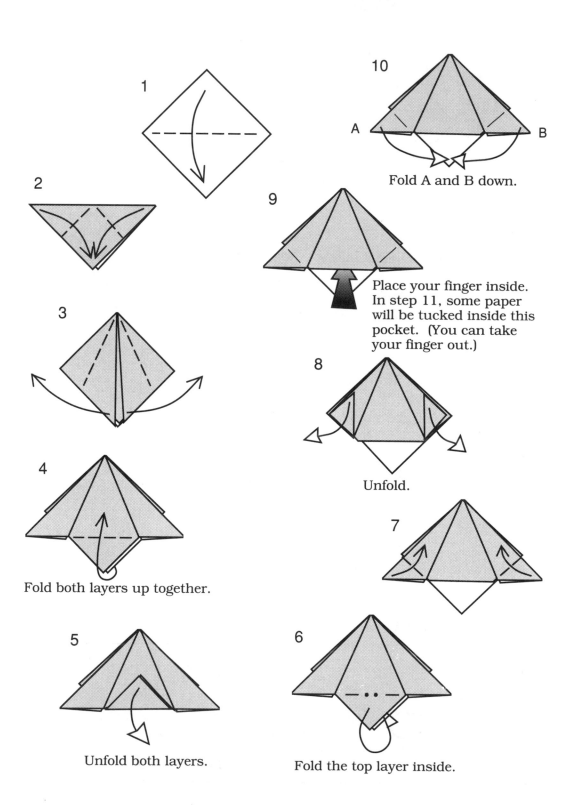

1

2

3

4

Fold both layers up together.

5

Unfold both layers.

6

Fold the top layer inside.

7

8

Unfold.

9

Place your finger inside. In step 11, some paper will be tucked inside this pocket. (You can take your finger out.)

10

A   B

Fold A and B down.

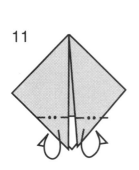

11

Tuck inside the pocket.

12

Tuck inside the pocket.

13

A   B

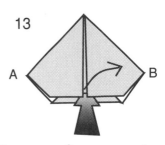

Place your finger - maybe your hand - all the way in to open the model and then flatten it so that A and B meet.

14

A   B

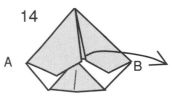

An intermediate step.

15

A

B

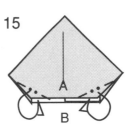

Fold the corners inside. Repeat behind.

16

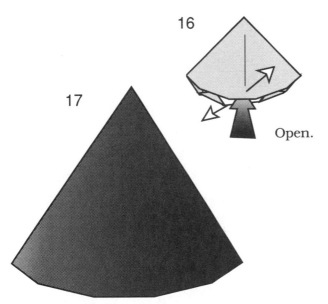

Open.

17

Mountain

18

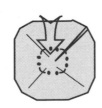

This is a top view of the mountain. To turn it into a volcano, push the top of it inside. This type of fold is called a sink fold.

19

Volcano

Cracked Dinosaur Egg

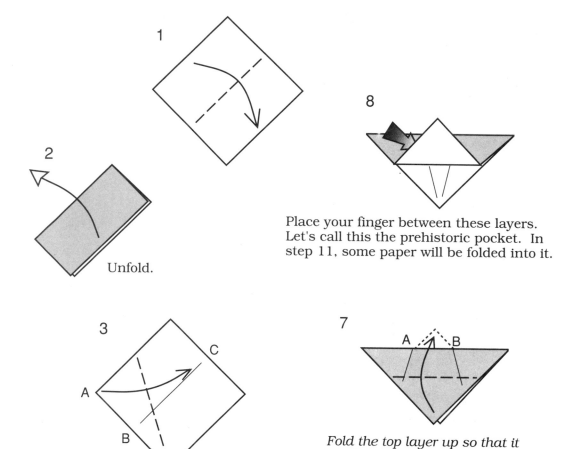

1

2

Unfold.

8

Place your finger between these layers. Let's call this the prehistoric pocket. In step 11, some paper will be folded into it.

3

C

A

B

Fold A to touch somewhere on line B-C.

7

A   B

Fold the top layer up so that it touches A and B. The dotted lines show where the paper will end.

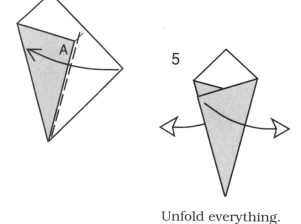

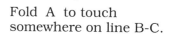

4

A

5

6

Unfold everything.

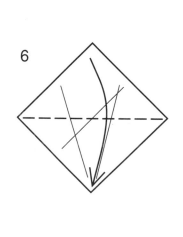

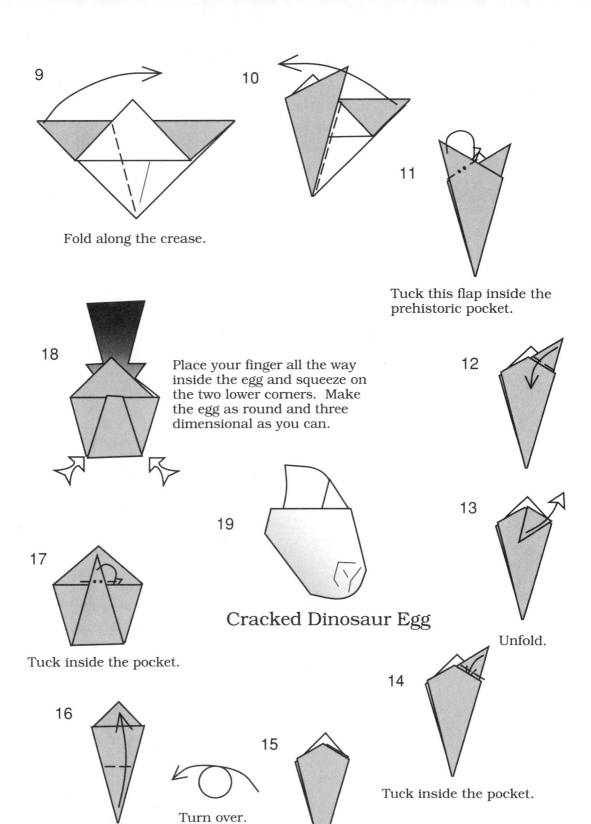

9

Fold along the crease.

10

11

Tuck this flap inside the prehistoric pocket.

12

13

Unfold.

14

Tuck inside the pocket.

18

Place your finger all the way inside the egg and squeeze on the two lower corners. Make the egg as round and three dimensional as you can.

19

Cracked Dinosaur Egg

17

Tuck inside the pocket.

16

15

Turn over.

Prehistoric Tree

Method 1

The simple way.

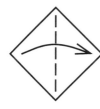

1

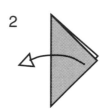

2

Unfold.

3

4

Unfold.

5

Kite fold, fold to the center line.

6

Unfold.

7

Kite fold and unfold.

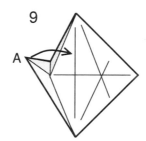

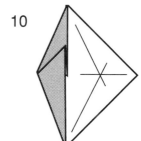

8

B

A

C

The folding and unfolding has been done to prepare for the rabbit ear fold. Using the creases, lift corner A up, fold it in half, and lay it down on line B-C.

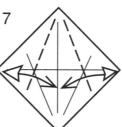

9

A

An intermediate step. Continue folding up.

10

A rabbit ear fold has just been formed. Repeat steps 8-9 on the right.

Method 2

The standard way.

1

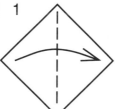

2

Two rabbit ears.

3

Fold behind.

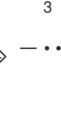

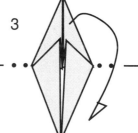

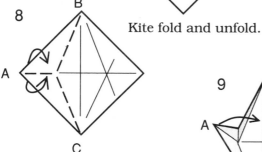

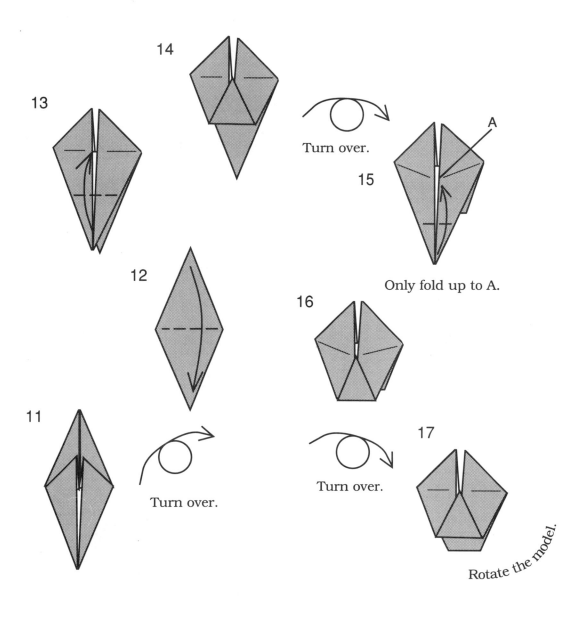

14

13

Turn over.

A

15

Only fold up to A.

12

16

11

Turn over.

Turn over.

17

Rotate the model.

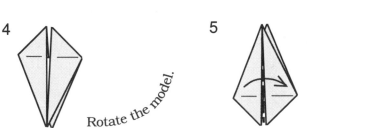

4

Rotate the model.

5

6

Outside reverse fold.

PREHISTORIC TREE

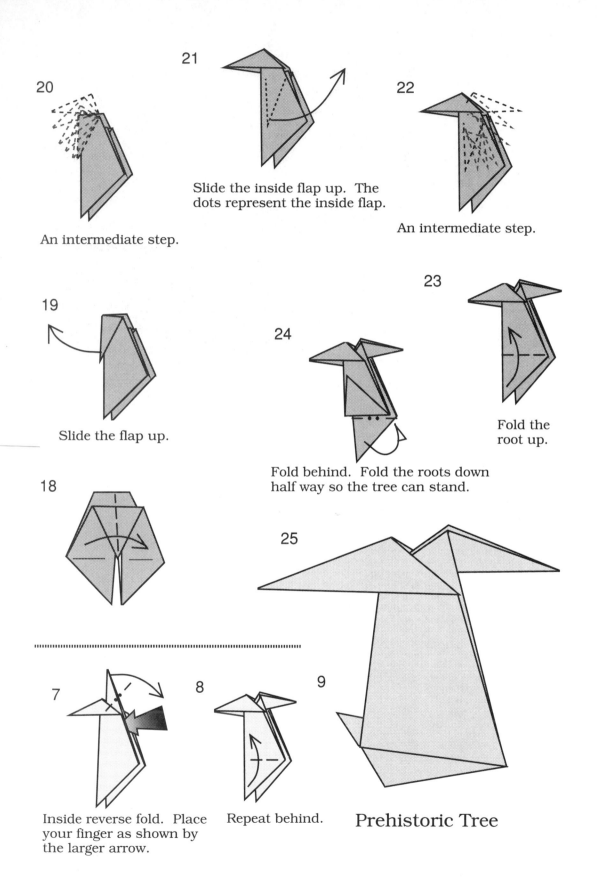

21

Slide the inside flap up. The dots represent the inside flap.

20

An intermediate step.

22

An intermediate step.

19

Slide the flap up.

23

Fold the root up.

24

Fold behind. Fold the roots down half way so the tree can stand.

18

25

7

Inside reverse fold. Place your finger as shown by the larger arrow.

8

Repeat behind.

9

Prehistoric Tree

The Bird Base

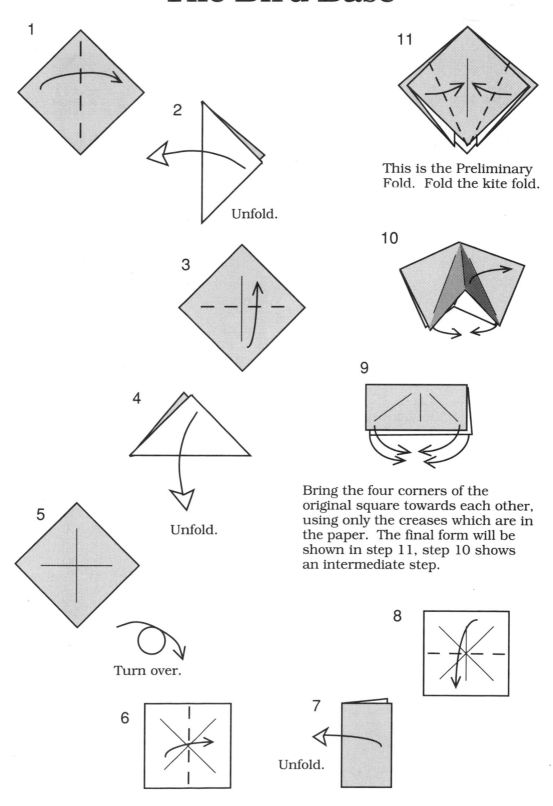

1

2

Unfold.

3

4

Unfold.

5

Turn over.

6

7

Unfold.

8

9

Bring the four corners of the original square towards each other, using only the creases which are in the paper. The final form will be shown in step 11, step 10 shows an intermediate step.

10

11

This is the Preliminary Fold. Fold the kite fold.

12

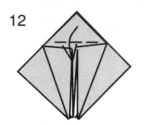

Fold the triangle down.

13

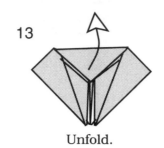

Unfold.

14

Unfold.

The petal fold is introduced. Step 18 shows the completed petal fold. This is a tricky fold! The idea is to fold the corner A up as high as it can go, which is well above corner B. Also, C and D will come together. Place your fingers as shown by the large arrows. You are only folding upon the creases which already exist. If you simply fold A to B then it will be wrong!

15

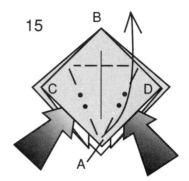

16

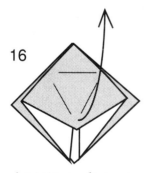

An intermediate step.

17

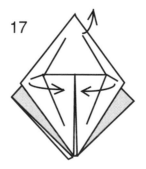

An intermediate step.

18

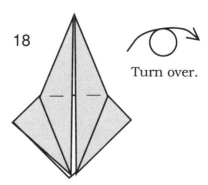

Turn over.

A completed petal fold.

PREHISTORIC ORIGAMI

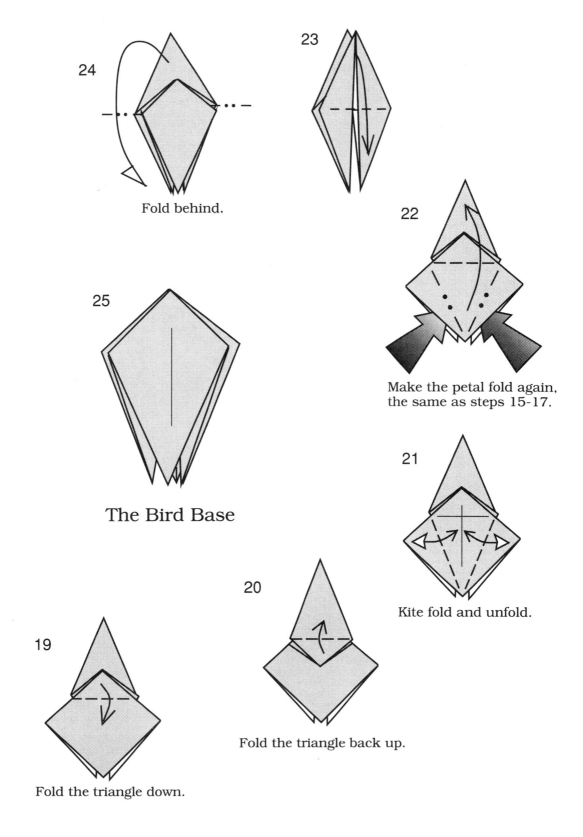

24

Fold behind.

23

22

Make the petal fold again,
the same as steps 15-17.

25

The Bird Base

21

Kite fold and unfold.

20

Fold the triangle back up.

19

Fold the triangle down.

Parasaurolophus

par-a-SAUR-oh-loaf-us

A swamp dwelling, Cretaceous plant eater, this dinosaur was 33 feet long. The webbed feet and bill were not the only similarities to ducks. The long tubular crest on the top of the head may have enabled it to honk like a goose. It had grinding teeth in the back of the mouth. Parasaurolophus means "almost crest head" and it may have been the female to Corythosaurus.

1

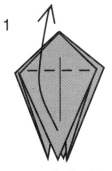

Begin with the Bird Base (page 23).

7

This three dimensional figure shows the rabbit ear in progress.

6

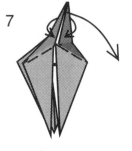

A rabbit ear will now be formed. To begin, fold the two sides of the tip towards each other. Step 8 shows the completed rabbit ear.

2

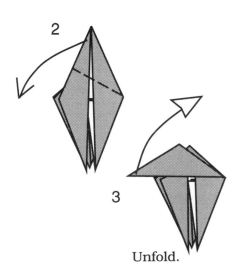

3

Unfold.

4

5

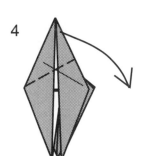

Unfold.

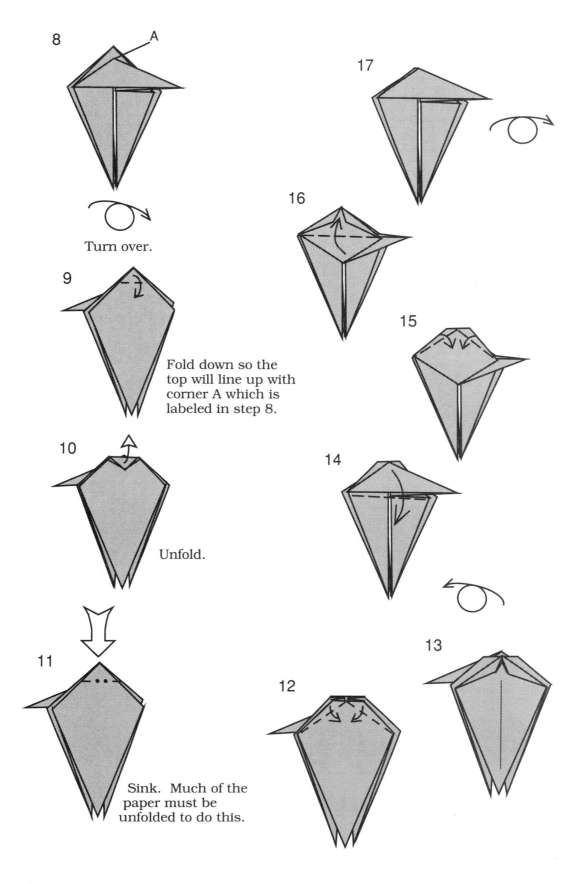

8

A

Turn over.

9

Fold down so the top will line up with corner A which is labeled in step 8.

10

Unfold.

11

Sink. Much of the paper must be unfolded to do this.

12

13

14

15

16

17

PARASAUROLOPHUS

18

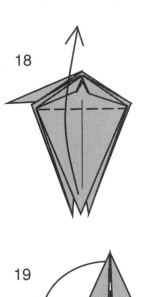

25

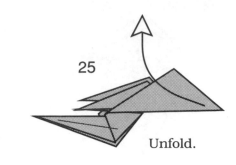

Unfold.

19

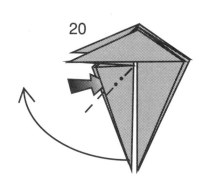

Rabbit ear, the
same as steps 2-8.

24

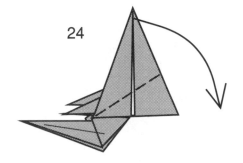

20

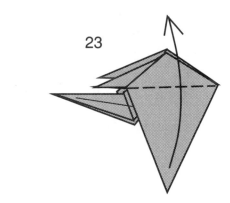

Reverse fold.

23

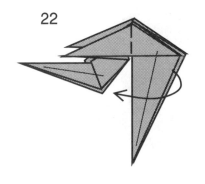

21

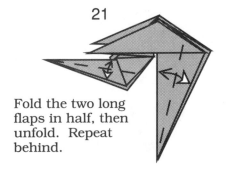

Fold the two long
flaps in half, then
unfold. Repeat
behind.

22

PREHISTORIC ORIGAMI

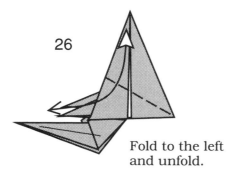

26

Fold to the left
and unfold.

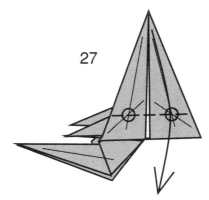

27

Fold down at the intersection
of the lines indicated by the
two circles.

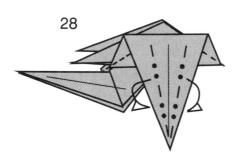

28

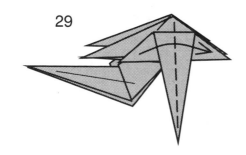

29

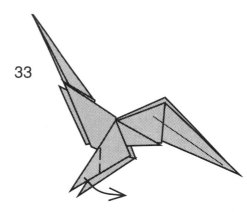

33

Repeat behind.

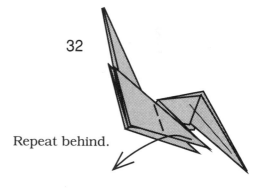

32

Repeat behind.

Rotate the model.

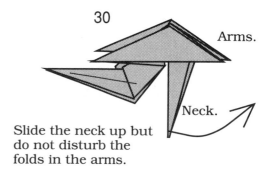

31

30

Arms.

Neck.

Slide the neck up but
do not disturb the
folds in the arms.

PARASAUROLOPHUS

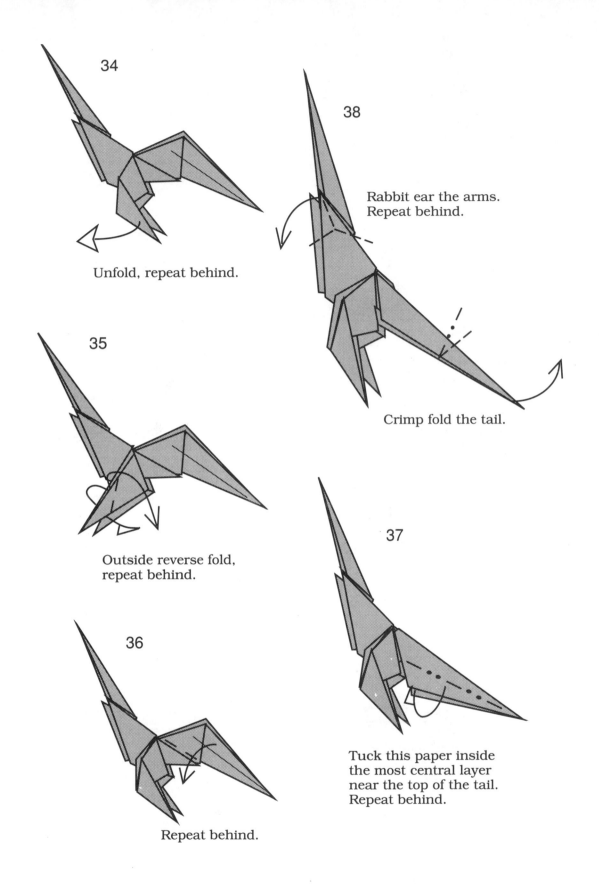

34

Unfold, repeat behind.

38

Rabbit ear the arms.
Repeat behind.

Crimp fold the tail.

35

Outside reverse fold,
repeat behind.

37

Tuck this paper inside
the most central layer
near the top of the tail.
Repeat behind.

36

Repeat behind.

PREHISTORIC ORIGAMI

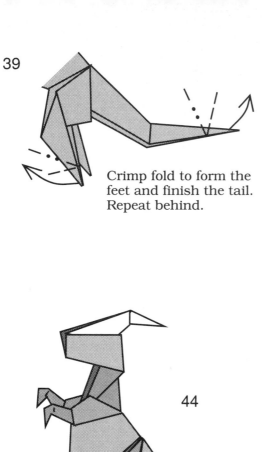

39

Crimp fold to form the feet and finish the tail. Repeat behind.

40

Crimp fold the arms. Repeat behind.

44

Parasaurolophus

41

Crimp fold to form the head. Fold the hand down. Repeat behind.

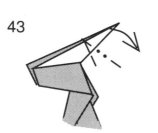

43

Crimp fold the crown.

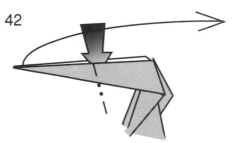

42

This asymmetric reverse fold will form the white crown.

Struthiomimus

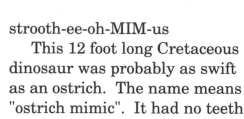

strooth-ee-oh-MIM-us

This 12 foot long Cretaceous dinosaur was probably as swift as an ostrich. The name means "ostrich mimic". It had no teeth in its beak and used its three-fingered hands to dig and grasp food. The tail helped it balance. Fossils were found in New Jersey and Canada.

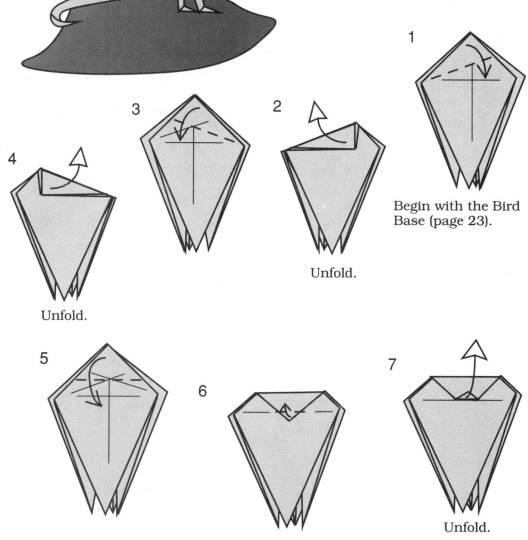

1

Begin with the Bird Base (page 23).

2

Unfold.

3

4

Unfold.

5

6

7

Unfold.

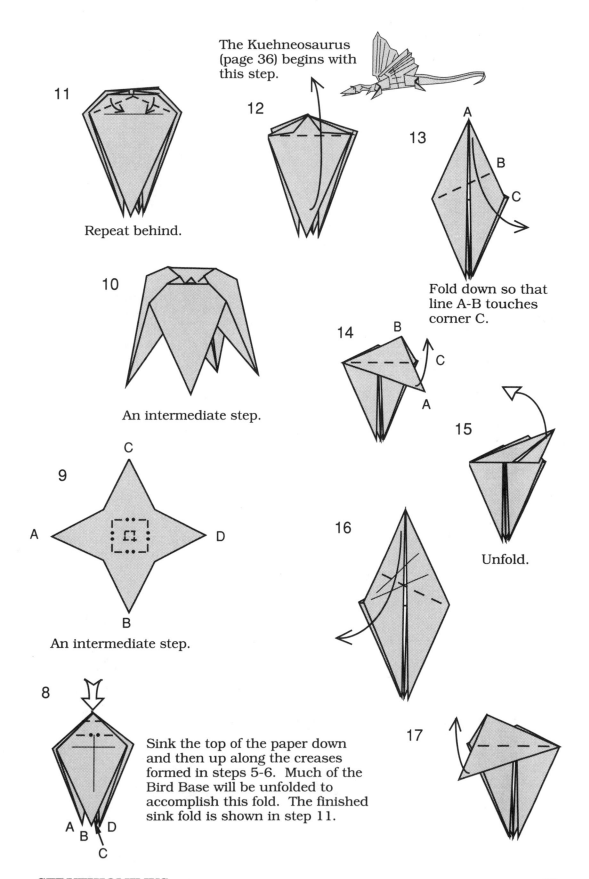

11

Repeat behind.

The Kuehneosaurus (page 36) begins with this step.

12

13

A
B
C

Fold down so that line A-B touches corner C.

10

An intermediate step.

14

B
C
A

15

Unfold.

9

C
A
D
B

An intermediate step.

16

8

A D
B
C

Sink the top of the paper down and then up along the creases formed in steps 5-6. Much of the Bird Base will be unfolded to accomplish this fold. The finished sink fold is shown in step 11.

17

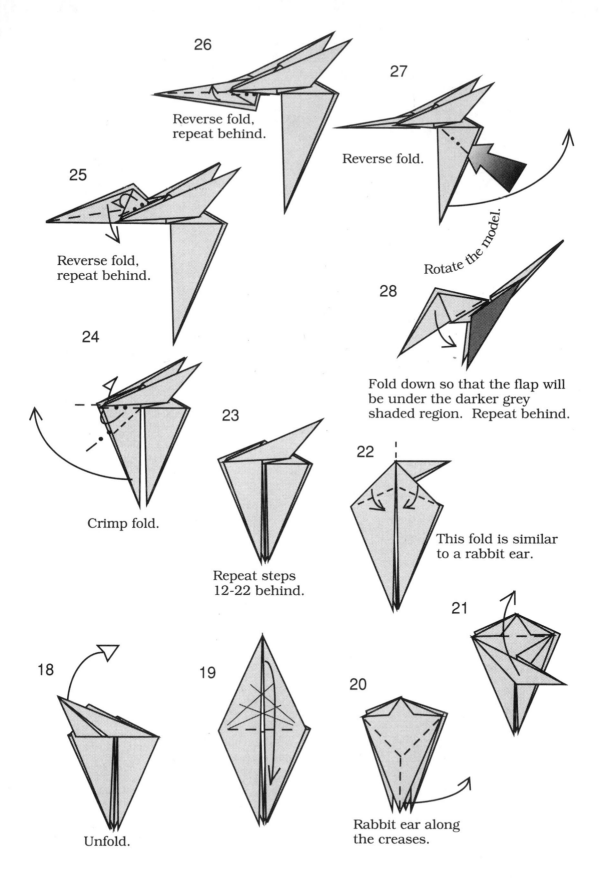

26

Reverse fold,
repeat behind.

27

Reverse fold.

Rotate the model.

25

Reverse fold,
repeat behind.

28

Fold down so that the flap will
be under the darker grey
shaded region. Repeat behind.

24

Crimp fold.

23

Repeat steps
12-22 behind.

22

This fold is similar
to a rabbit ear.

21

18

Unfold.

19

20

Rabbit ear along
the creases.

PREHISTORIC ORIGAMI

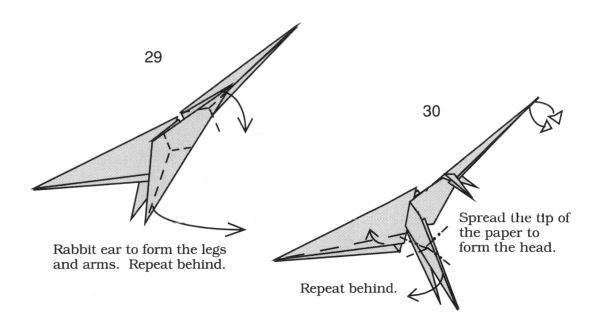

29

Rabbit ear to form the legs and arms. Repeat behind.

30

Spread the tip of the paper to form the head.

Repeat behind.

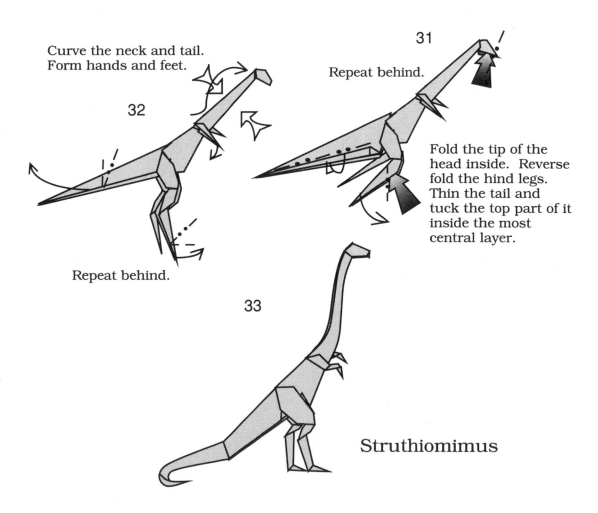

Curve the neck and tail. Form hands and feet.

32

Repeat behind.

31

Repeat behind.

Fold the tip of the head inside. Reverse fold the hind legs. Thin the tail and tuck the top part of it inside the most central layer.

33

Struthiomimus

Kuehneosaurus

KU-nee-oh-saw-rus

This gliding lizard was 10 to 12 inches long and shared the Triassic period with some of the early dinosaurs. It probably climbed trees, spread its hollow ribs, and glided to earth. The ribs were covered with a thin skin. Insects were its favorite food.

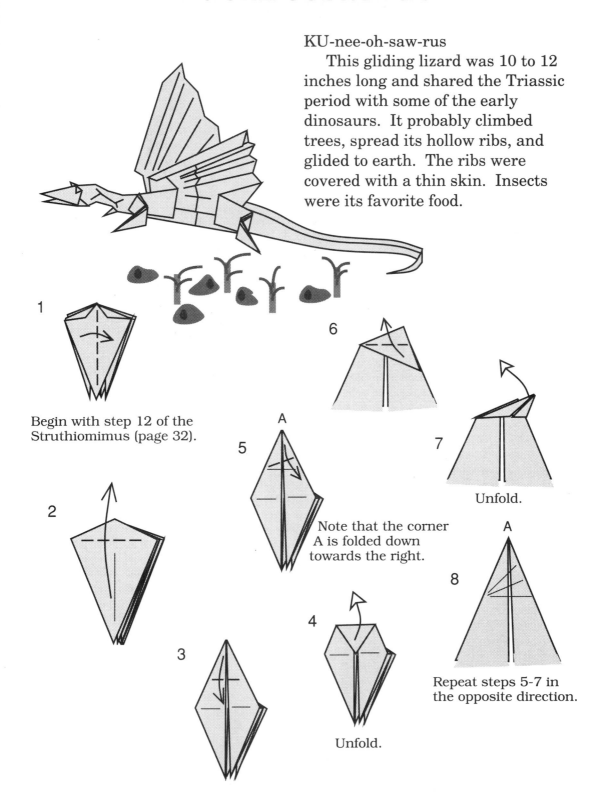

1

Begin with step 12 of the Struthiomimus (page 32).

2

3

4

Unfold.

5

A

Note that the corner A is folded down towards the right.

6

7

Unfold.

8

A

Repeat steps 5-7 in the opposite direction.

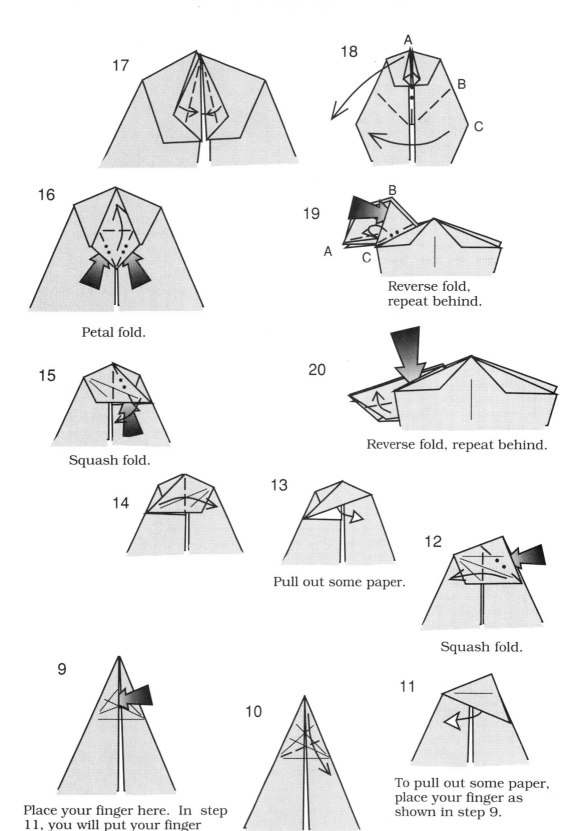

17

18

A

B

C

16

Petal fold.

19

B

A

C

Reverse fold,
repeat behind.

15

Squash fold.

20

Reverse fold, repeat behind.

14

13

Pull out some paper.

12

Squash fold.

9

Place your finger here. In step 11, you will put your finger there to pull out some paper.

10

11

To pull out some paper, place your finger as shown in step 9.

21

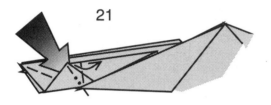

Squash fold. Repeat behind.

22

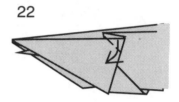

Form the eye, repeat behind.

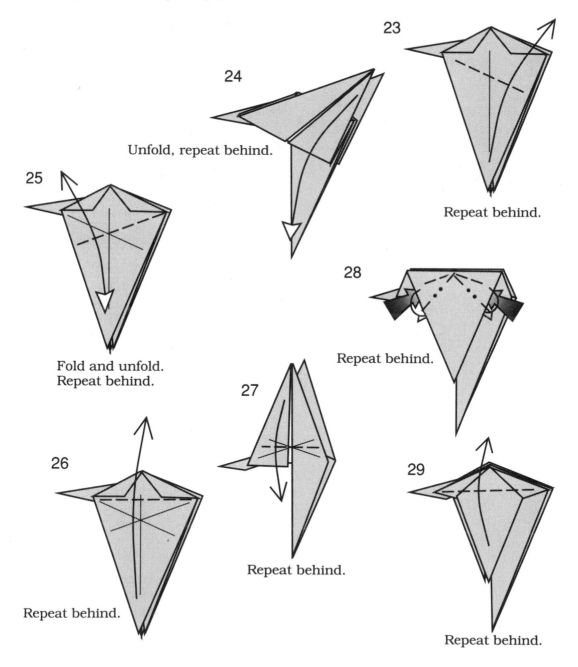

23

Repeat behind.

24

Unfold, repeat behind.

25

Fold and unfold.
Repeat behind.

26

Repeat behind.

27

Repeat behind.

28

Repeat behind.

29

Repeat behind.

PREHISTORIC ORIGAMI

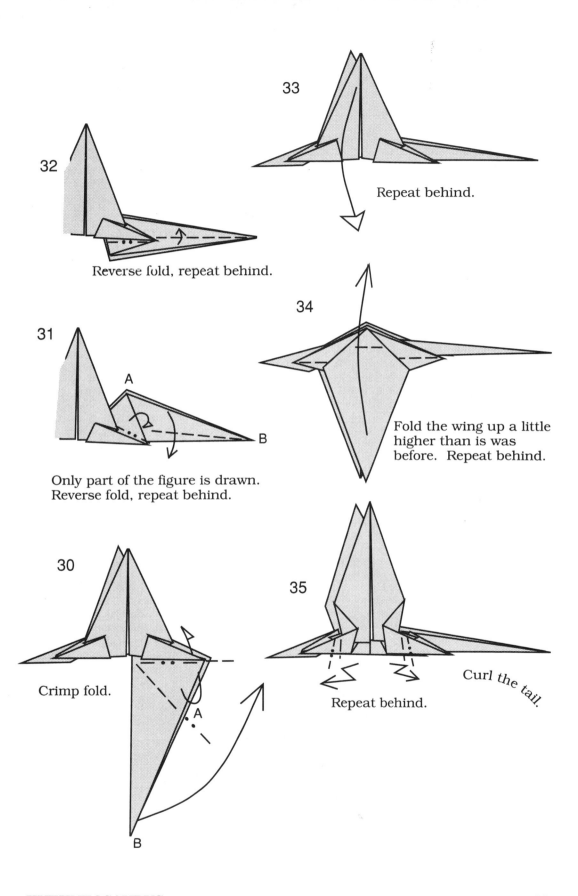

32

Reverse fold, repeat behind.

33

Repeat behind.

31

A

B

Only part of the figure is drawn.
Reverse fold, repeat behind.

34

Fold the wing up a little
higher than is was
before. Repeat behind.

30

Crimp fold.

A

B

35

Repeat behind.

Curl the tail.

36

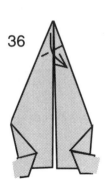

Repeat behind.

37

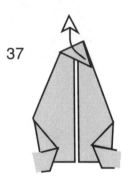

Unfold, repeat behind.

38

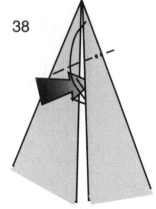

Tuck the tip inside.
Repeat behind.

40

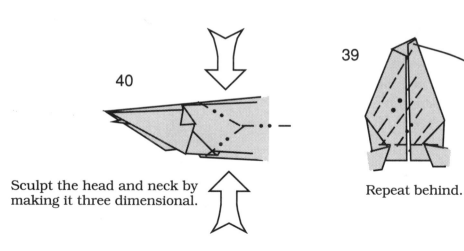

Sculpt the head and neck by
making it three dimensional.

39

Repeat behind.

41

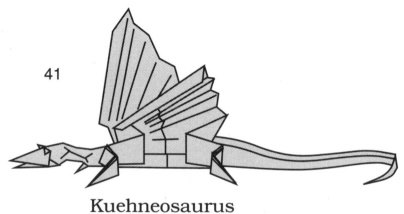

Kuehneosaurus

Archaeopteryx

are-key-OP-ter-ix

Once thought to be the first bird, this animal was more like a dinosaur than some of the Mesozoic animals that took to the air. It had solid bones, teeth in its beak, and was not able to fly or glide. It ran around the Jurassic forest floor catching insects. It was the size of a crow and was covered with feathers and scales. Archaeopteryx means "ancient wing".

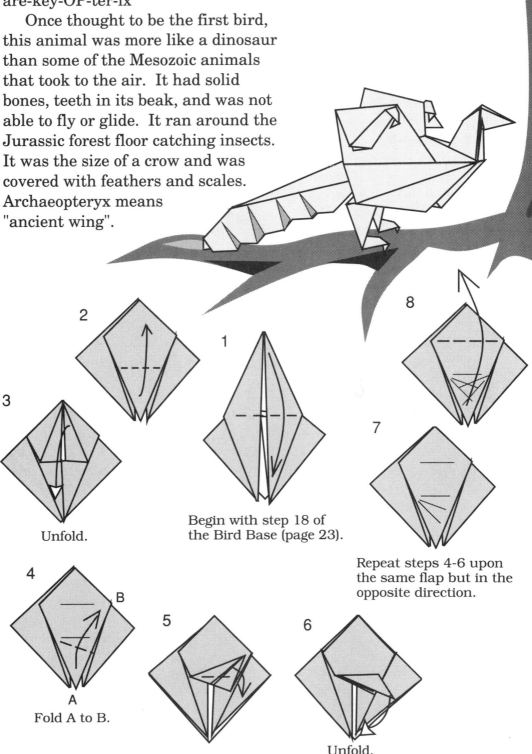

2

1

Begin with step 18 of the Bird Base (page 23).

3

Unfold.

8

7

Repeat steps 4-6 upon the same flap but in the opposite direction.

4

B

A

Fold A to B.

5

6

Unfold.

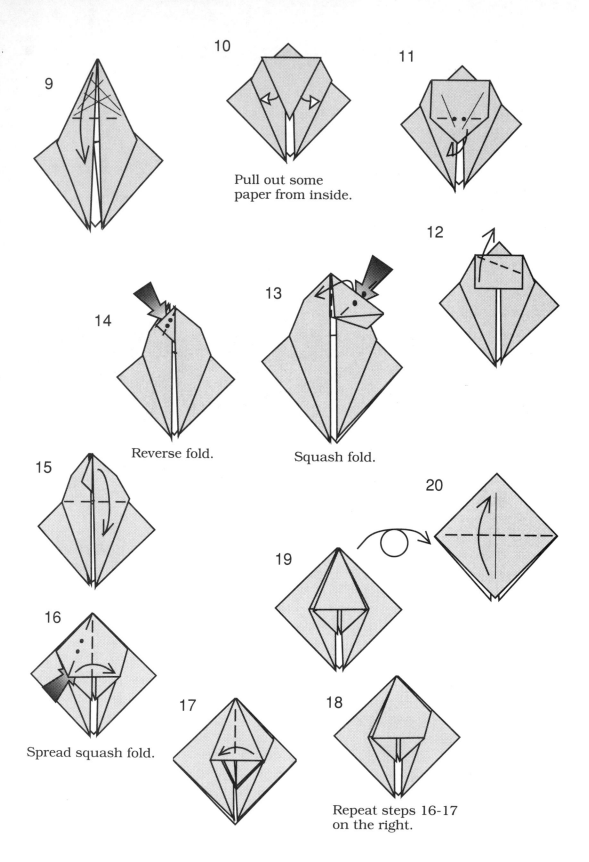

9

10

Pull out some
paper from inside.

11

12

13

Squash fold.

14

Reverse fold.

15

16

Spread squash fold.

17

18

Repeat steps 16-17
on the right.

19

20

　　　　　　　　　　　　　　PREHISTORIC ORIGAMI

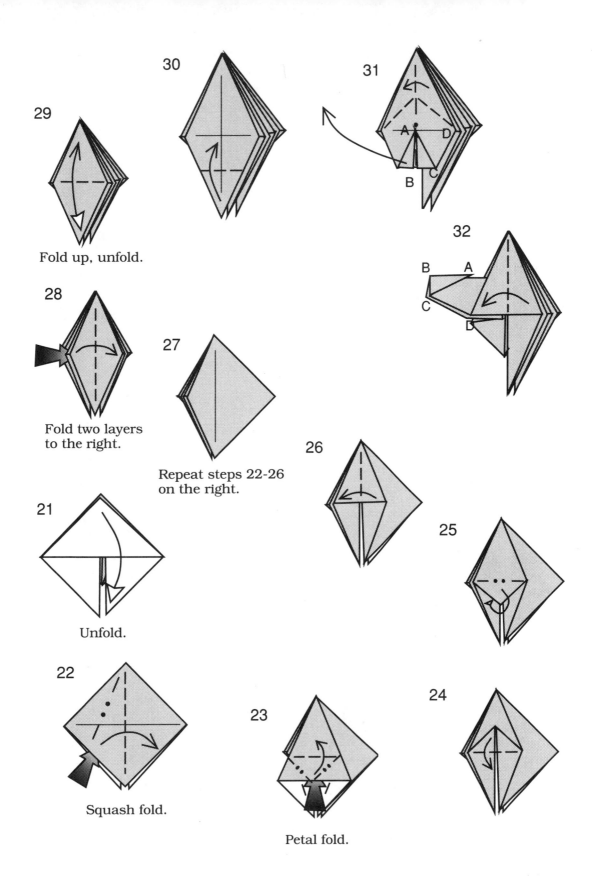

29

Fold up, unfold.

30

31

32

28

Fold two layers
to the right.

27

Repeat steps 22-26
on the right.

26

25

21

Unfold.

22

Squash fold.

23

Petal fold.

24

ARCHAEOPTERYX

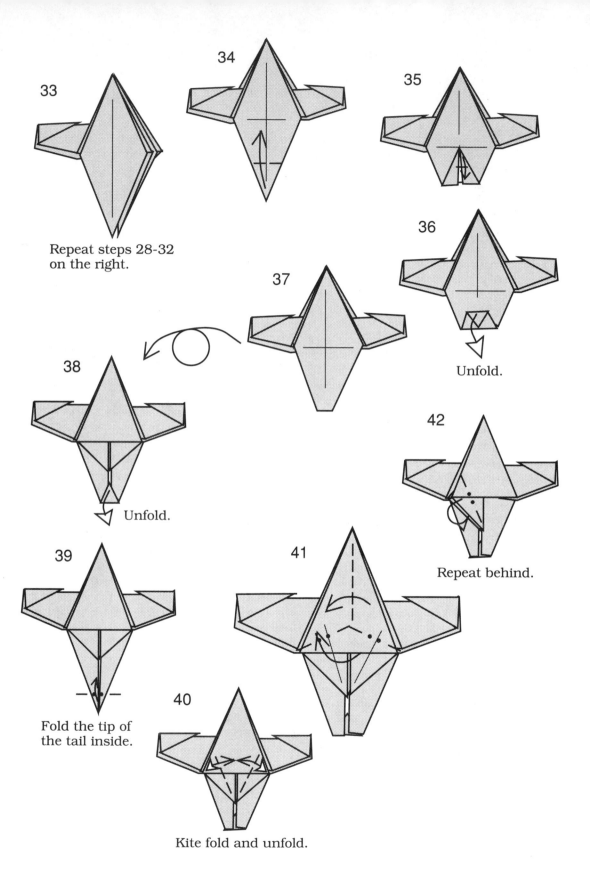

33

34

35

Repeat steps 28-32
on the right.

37

36

Unfold.

38

Unfold.

39

41

42

Repeat behind.

Fold the tip of
the tail inside.

40

Kite fold and unfold.

PREHISTORIC ORIGAMI

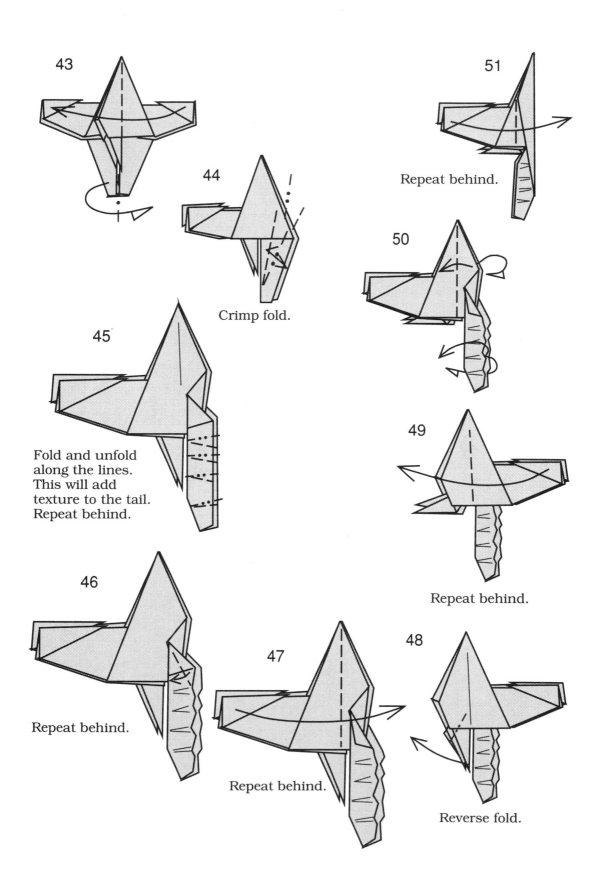

43

44

Crimp fold.

45

Fold and unfold
along the lines.
This will add
texture to the tail.
Repeat behind.

46

Repeat behind.

47

Repeat behind.

48

Reverse fold.

49

Repeat behind.

50

51

Repeat behind.

ARCHAEOPTERYX

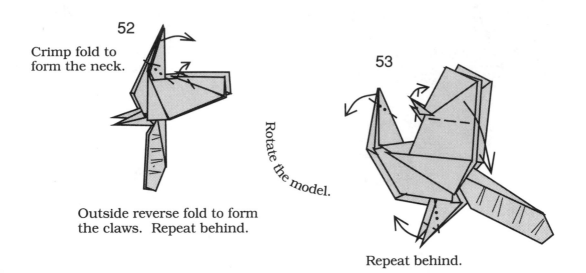

52

Crimp fold to form the neck.

Rotate the model.

Outside reverse fold to form the claws. Repeat behind.

53

Repeat behind.

55

Foot.

Reverse fold, repeat behind.

54

Head.

Fold two layers down, repeat behind.

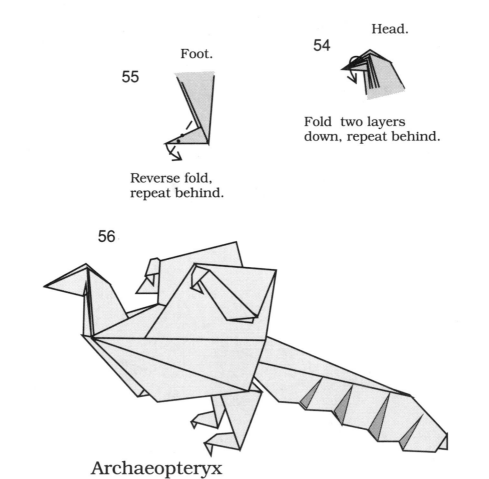

56

Archaeopteryx

Pterodactylus

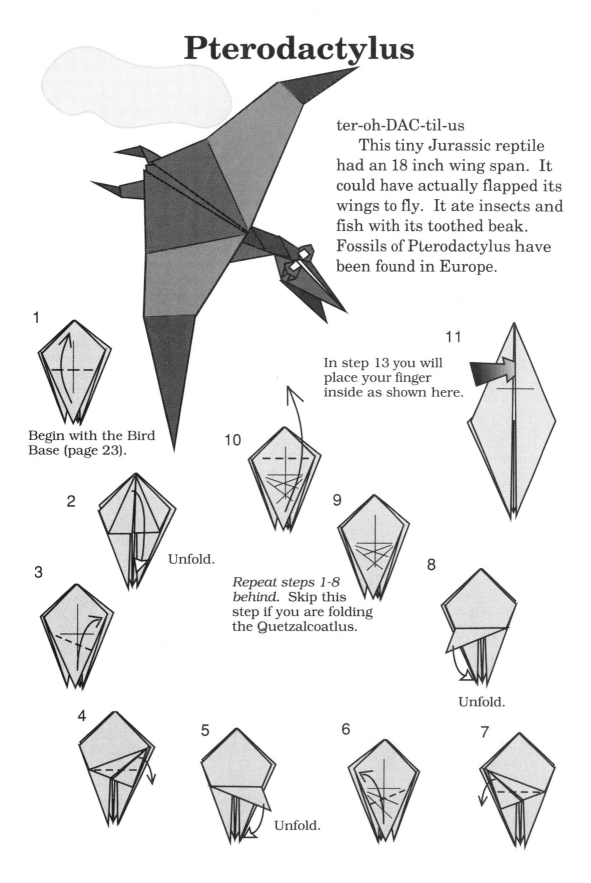

ter-oh-DAC-til-us

This tiny Jurassic reptile had an 18 inch wing span. It could have actually flapped its wings to fly. It ate insects and fish with its toothed beak. Fossils of Pterodactylus have been found in Europe.

1

Begin with the Bird Base (page 23).

2

Unfold.

3

4

5

Unfold.

6

7

8

Unfold.

9

10

Repeat steps 1-8 behind. Skip this step if you are folding the Quetzalcoatlus.

11

In step 13 you will place your finger inside as shown here.

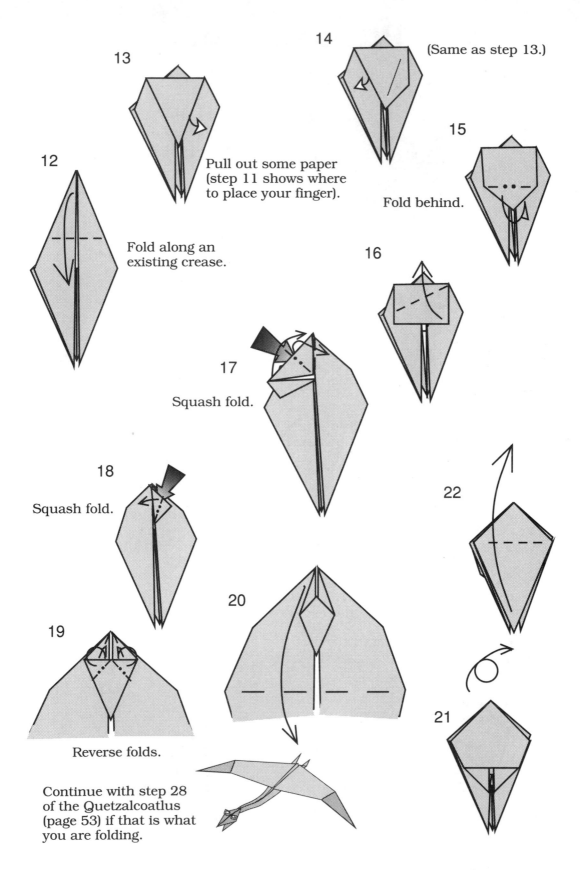

13

14 (Same as step 13.)

15

Pull out some paper (step 11 shows where to place your finger).

Fold behind.

12

Fold along an existing crease.

16

17

Squash fold.

18

Squash fold.

22

20

19

Reverse folds.

21

Continue with step 28 of the Quetzalcoatlus (page 53) if that is what you are folding.

PREHISTORIC ORIGAMI

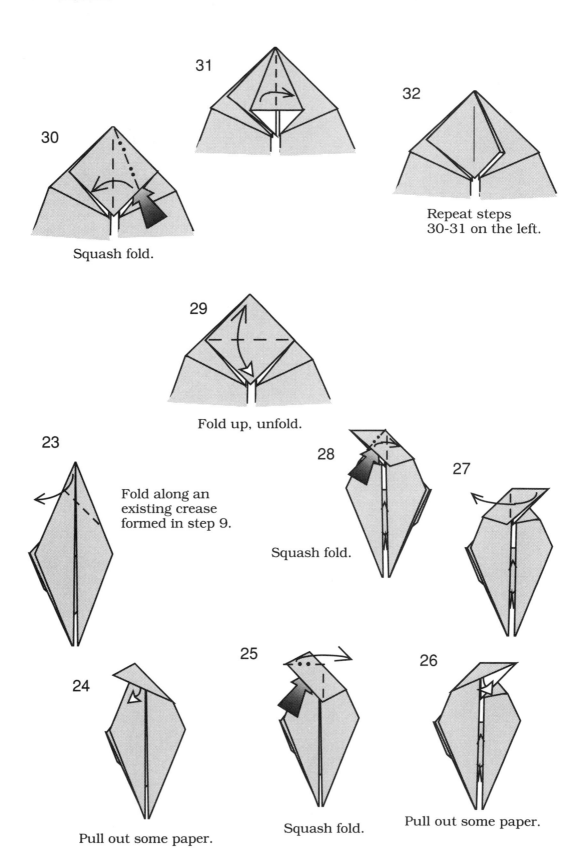

30

Squash fold.

31

32

Repeat steps
30-31 on the left.

29

Fold up, unfold.

23

Fold along an
existing crease
formed in step 9.

28

Squash fold.

27

24

Pull out some paper.

25

Squash fold.

26

Pull out some paper.

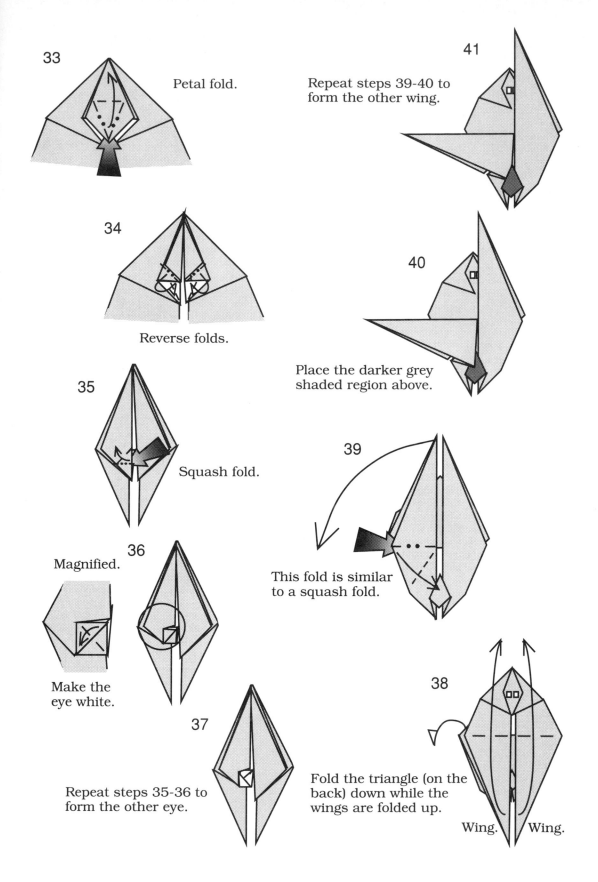

33 Petal fold.

34 Reverse folds.

35 Squash fold.

Magnified.

36

Make the
eye white.

37

Repeat steps 35-36 to
form the other eye.

41 Repeat steps 39-40 to
form the other wing.

40

Place the darker grey
shaded region above.

39

This fold is similar
to a squash fold.

38

Fold the triangle (on the
back) down while the
wings are folded up.

Wing.   Wing.

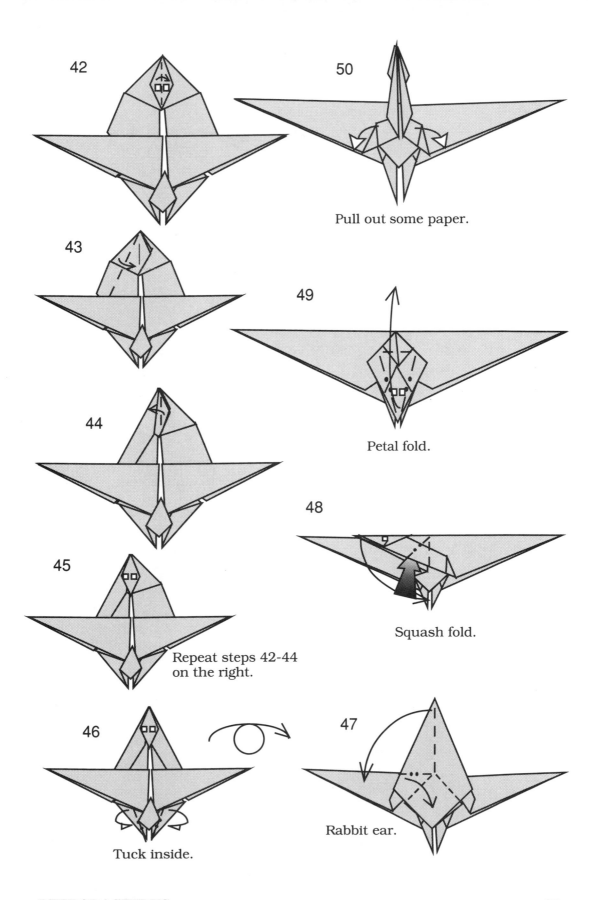

42

50

Pull out some paper.

43

49

Petal fold.

44

48

Squash fold.

45

Repeat steps 42-44 on the right.

46

Tuck inside.

47

Rabbit ear.

PTERODACTYLUS

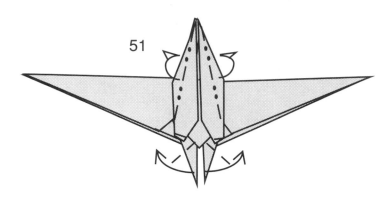

51

52

Shape the head.

Shape the wings with simple
valley and mountain folds.

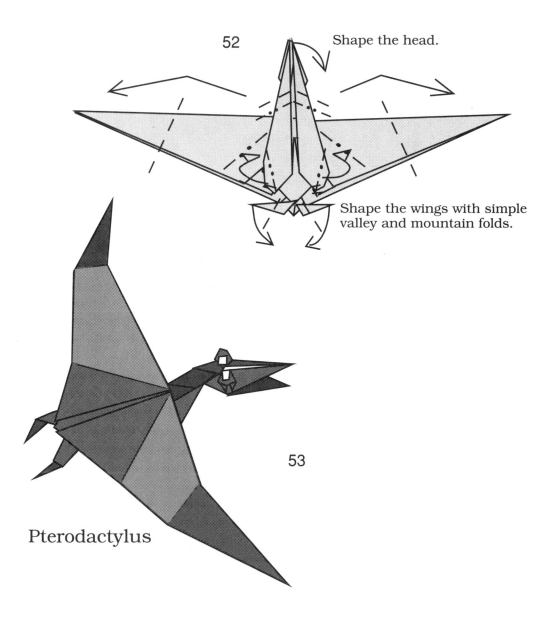

53

Pterodactylus

Quetzalcoatlus

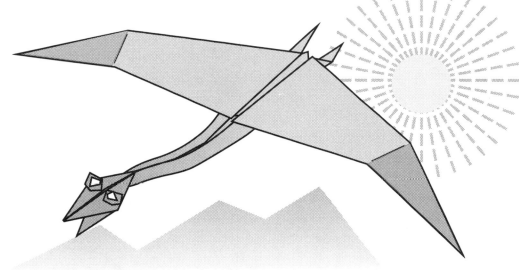

ket-SAT-co-at-til-us

Named for the Aztec God who was represented by a feathered serpent, this was the largest gliding reptile ever discovered. It had a 40 foot wing span. Because of its hollow bones, it was light enough to soar over Cretaceous seas for fish. Fossils were found in Texas.

1

2

Unfold.

3

4

Unfold.

5

6

Unfold.

7

8

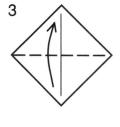

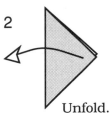

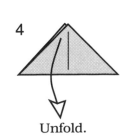

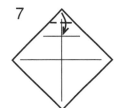

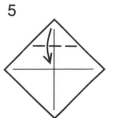

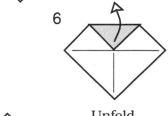

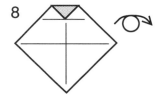

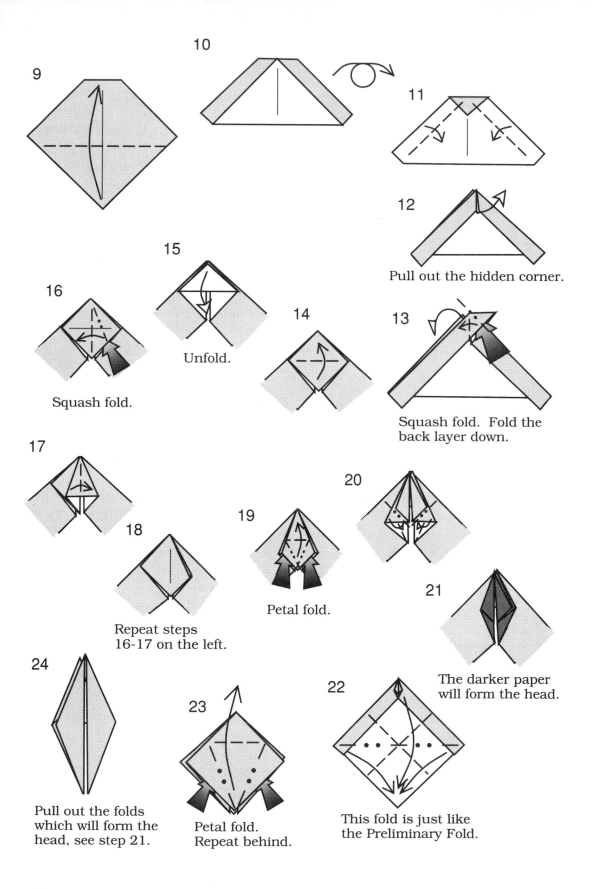

9

10

11

12

Pull out the hidden corner.

13

Squash fold. Fold the back layer down.

14

15

Unfold.

16

Squash fold.

17

18

Repeat steps 16-17 on the left.

19

Petal fold.

20

21

The darker paper will form the head.

22

This fold is just like the Preliminary Fold.

23

Petal fold. Repeat behind.

24

Pull out the folds which will form the head, see step 21.

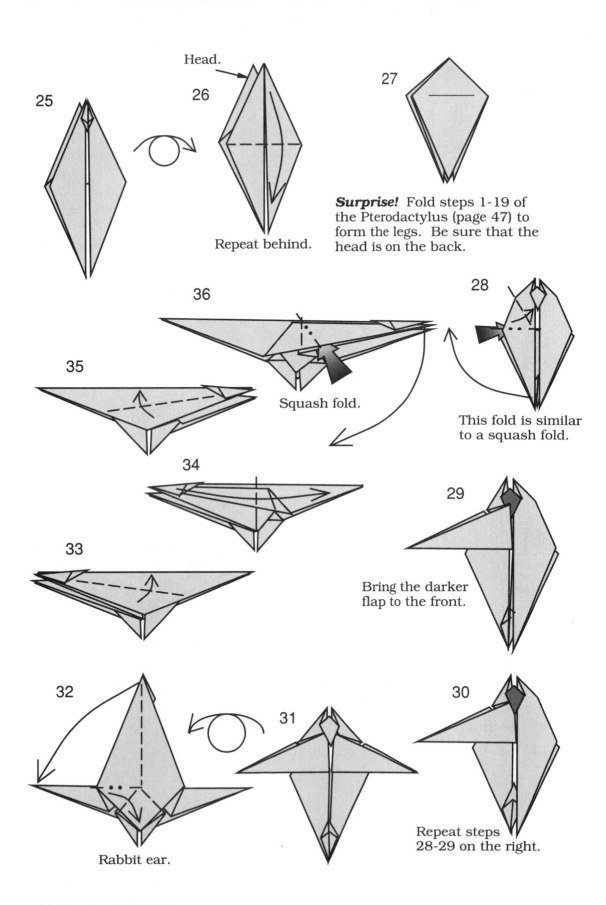

25

26

Head.

Repeat behind.

27

Surprise! Fold steps 1-19 of the Pterodactylus (page 47) to form the legs. Be sure that the head is on the back.

28

This fold is similar to a squash fold.

36

Squash fold.

35

34

29

Bring the darker flap to the front.

33

32

31

30

Repeat steps 28-29 on the right.

Rabbit ear.

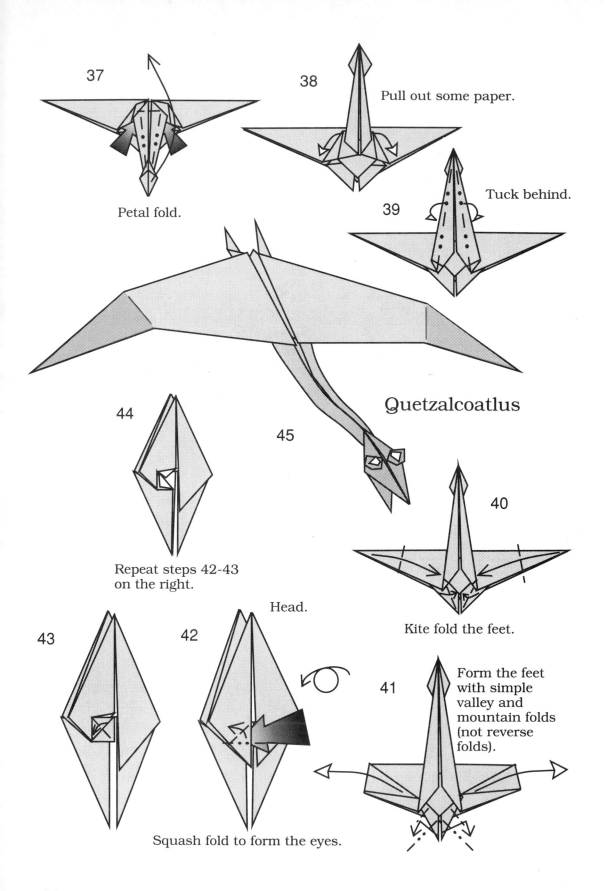

37

Petal fold.

38

Pull out some paper.

Tuck behind.

39

Quetzalcoatlus

44

Repeat steps 42-43
on the right.

45

40

Kite fold the feet.

Head.

43

42

41

Form the feet
with simple
valley and
mountain folds
(not reverse
folds).

Squash fold to form the eyes.

PREHISTORIC ORIGAMI

The Frog Base

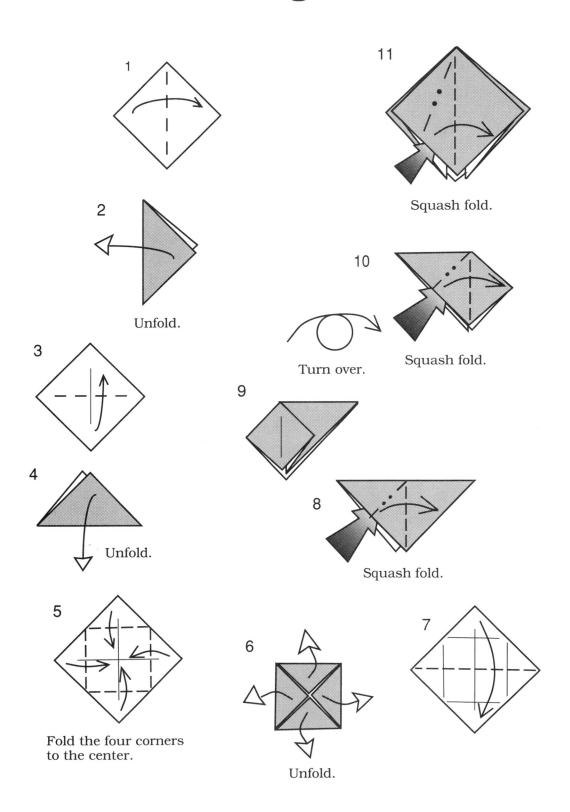

1

2

Unfold.

3

4

Unfold.

5

Fold the four corners
to the center.

6

Unfold.

7

8

Squash fold.

9

10

Turn over.

Squash fold.

11

Squash fold.

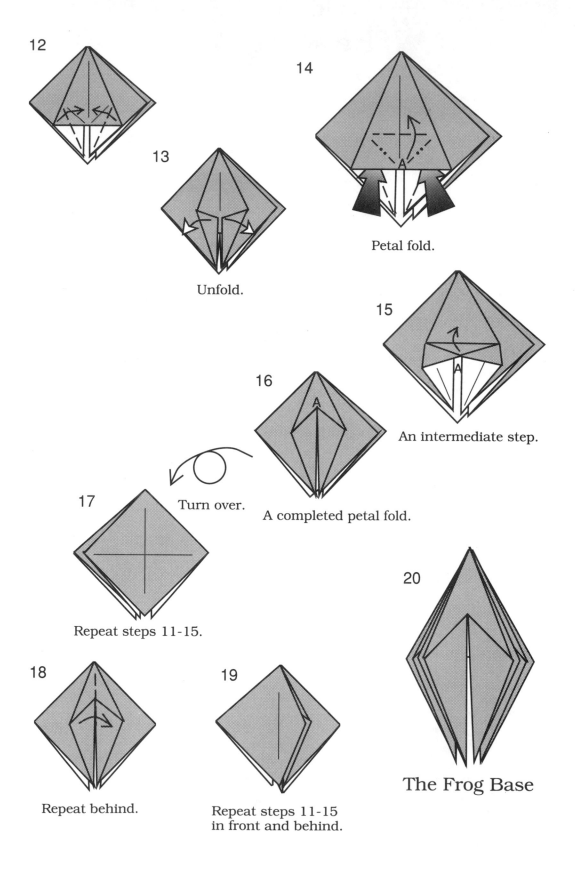

12

13

Unfold.

14

Petal fold.

15

An intermediate step.

16

A completed petal fold.

Turn over.

17

Repeat steps 11-15.

18

Repeat behind.

19

Repeat steps 11-15
in front and behind.

20

The Frog Base

Rhamphorynchus

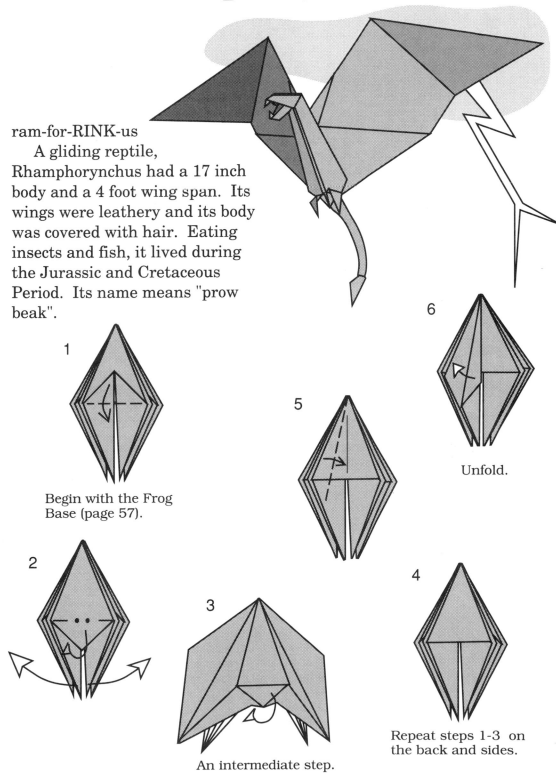

ram-for-RINK-us

A gliding reptile, Rhamphorynchus had a 17 inch body and a 4 foot wing span. Its wings were leathery and its body was covered with hair. Eating insects and fish, it lived during the Jurassic and Cretaceous Period. Its name means "prow beak".

1

Begin with the Frog Base (page 57).

2

3

An intermediate step.

4

Repeat steps 1-3 on the back and sides.

5

6

Unfold.

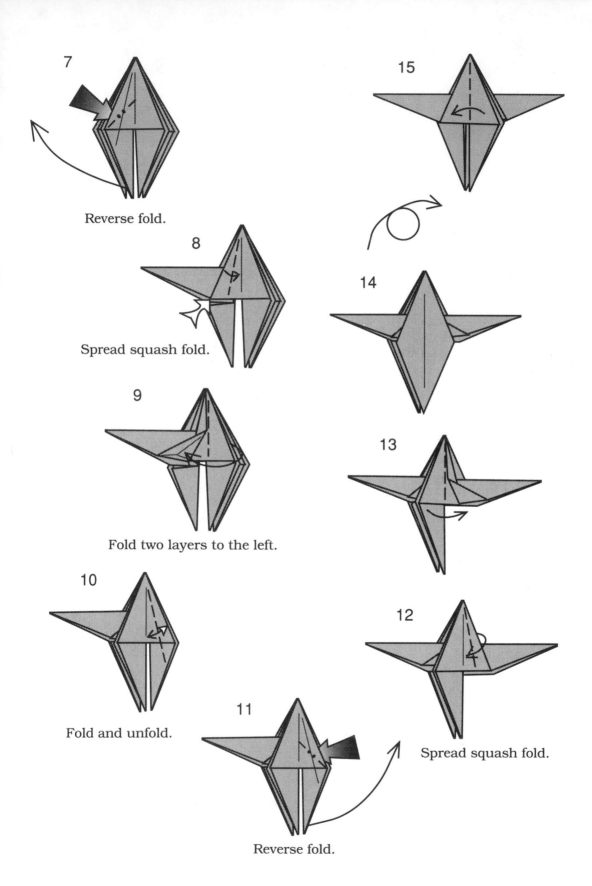

7

Reverse fold.

8

Spread squash fold.

9

Fold two layers to the left.

10

Fold and unfold.

11

Reverse fold.

12

Spread squash fold.

13

14

15

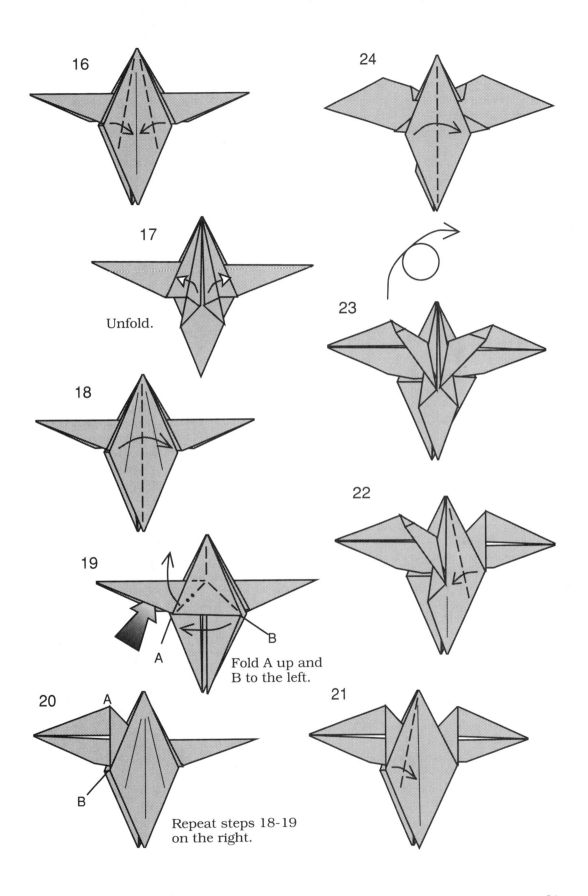

16

17

Unfold.

18

19

Fold A up and
B to the left.

A

B

20

A

B

Repeat steps 18-19
on the right.

21

22

23

24

RHAMPHORYNCHUS

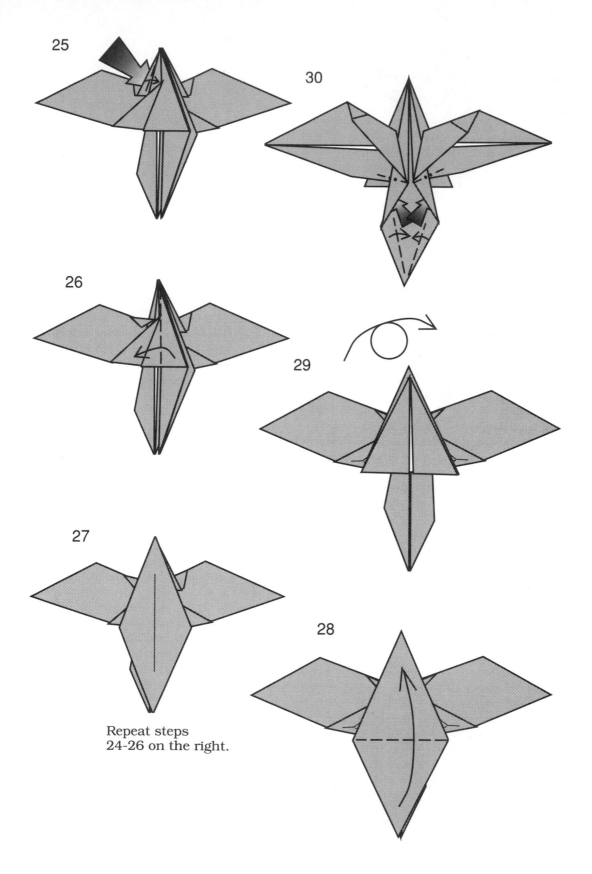

25

30

26

29

27

Repeat steps
24-26 on the right.

28

PREHISTORIC ORIGAMI

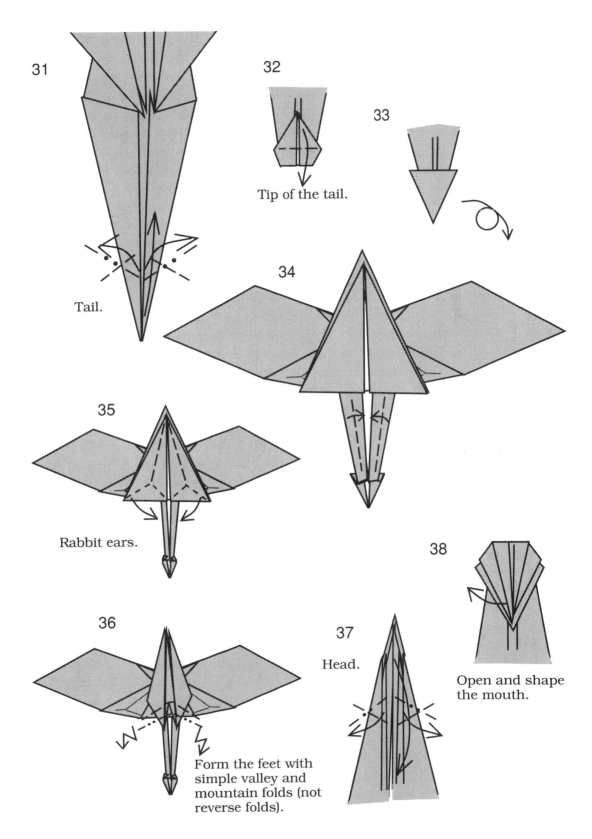

31

32

Tip of the tail.

33

Tail.

34

35

Rabbit ears.

38

36

37

Head.

Open and shape
the mouth.

Form the feet with
simple valley and
mountain folds (not
reverse folds).

RHAMPHORYNCHUS

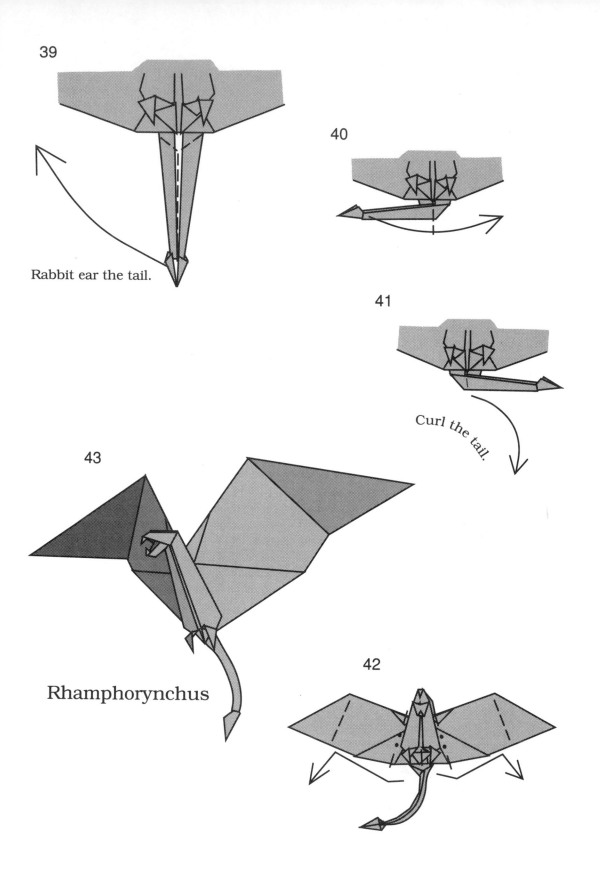

39

Rabbit ear the tail.

40

41

Curl the tail.

43

Rhamphorynchus

42

Pteranodon

ter-RAN-oh-don

With a 20 foot wing span, this gliding reptile swooped over Cretaceous seas picking up fish to eat. Its name means "toothless wing". The skin stretching across its "wings" was probably covered with hair. It glided off ocean cliffs in the western U.S.

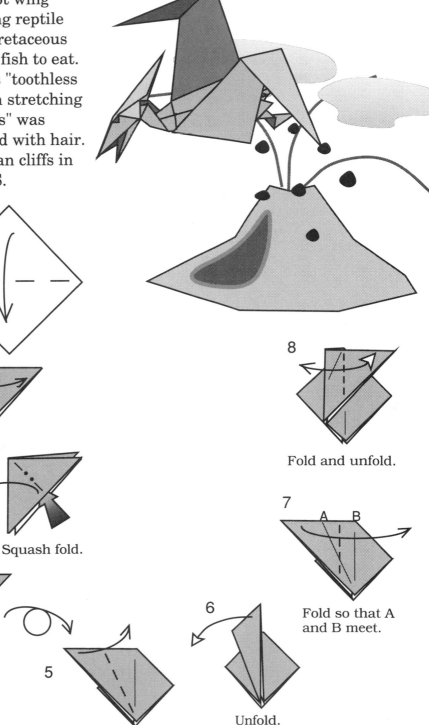

1

2

3

Squash fold.

4

5

6

Unfold.

7

Fold so that A and B meet.

8

Fold and unfold.

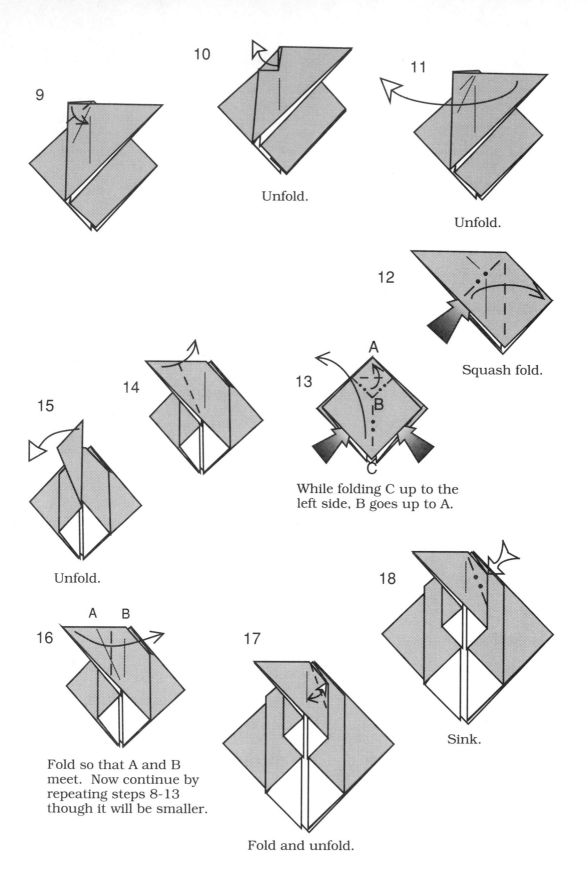

9

10

Unfold.

11

Unfold.

12

Squash fold.

13

A

B

C

While folding C up to the left side, B goes up to A.

14

15

Unfold.

16

A B

Fold so that A and B meet. Now continue by repeating steps 8-13 though it will be smaller.

17

Fold and unfold.

18

Sink.

PREHISTORIC ORIGAMI

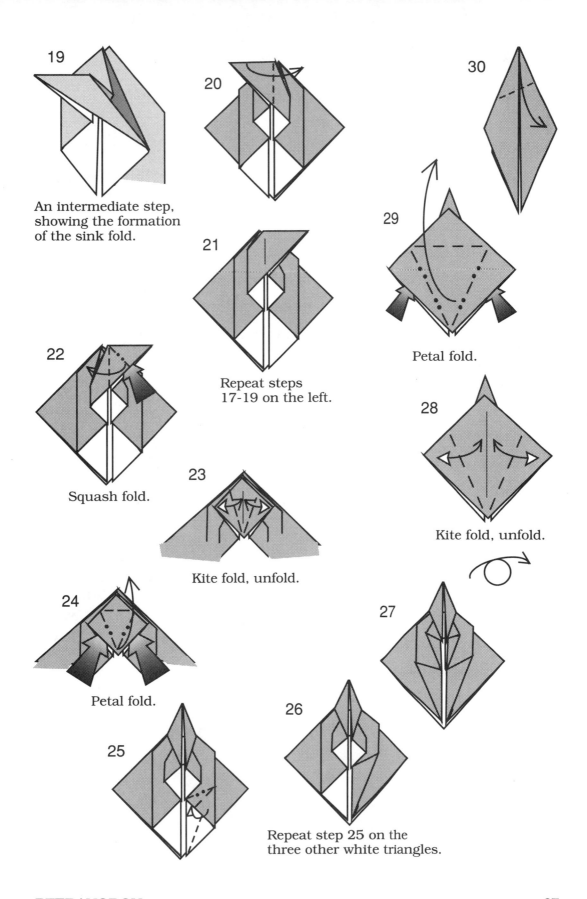

19

An intermediate step,
showing the formation
of the sink fold.

20

21

Repeat steps
17-19 on the left.

22

Squash fold.

23

Kite fold, unfold.

24

Petal fold.

25

26

Repeat step 25 on the
three other white triangles.

27

28

Kite fold, unfold.

29

Petal fold.

30

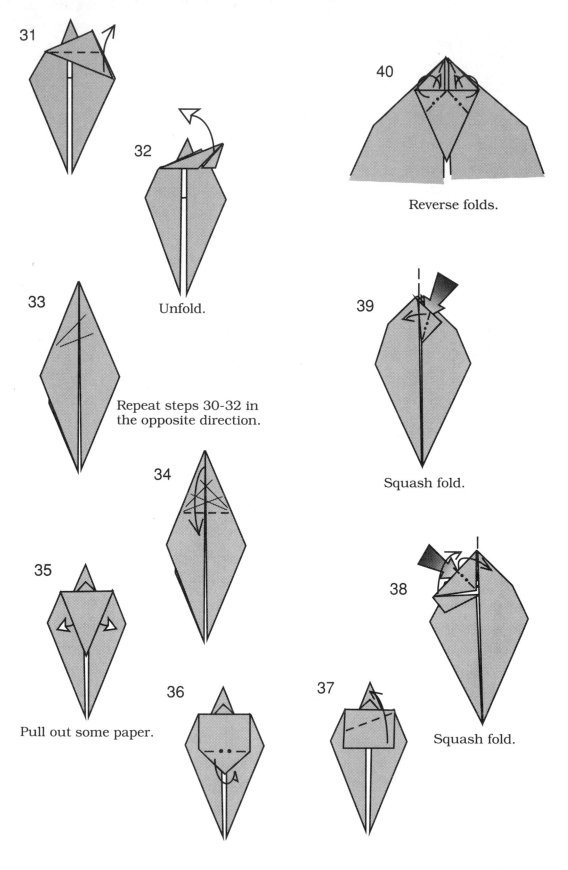

31

32

Unfold.

33

Repeat steps 30-32 in
the opposite direction.

34

35

Pull out some paper.

36

37

38

Squash fold.

39

Squash fold.

40

Reverse folds.

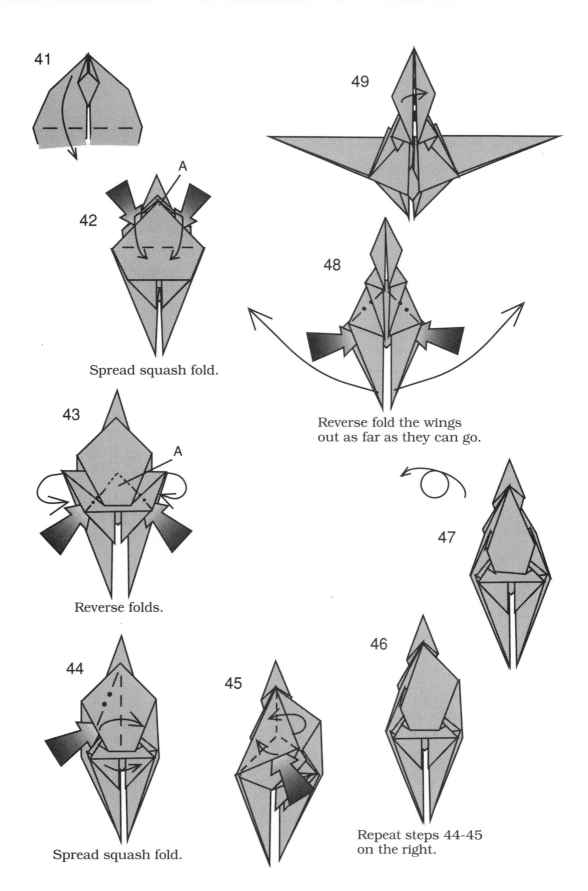

41

42

Spread squash fold.

43

Reverse folds.

44

Spread squash fold.

45

46

Repeat steps 44-45
on the right.

47

48

Reverse fold the wings
out as far as they can go.

49

A

A

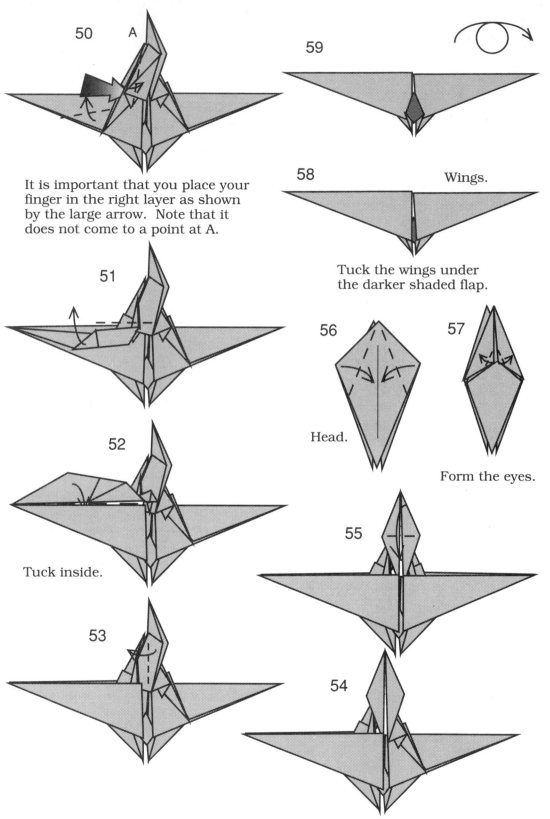

50 A

It is important that you place your
finger in the right layer as shown
by the large arrow. Note that it
does not come to a point at A.

51

52

Tuck inside.

53

59

58 Wings.

Tuck the wings under
the darker shaded flap.

56 **57**

Head.

Form the eyes.

55

54

Repeat steps 49-53 on the right.

PREHISTORIC ORIGAMI

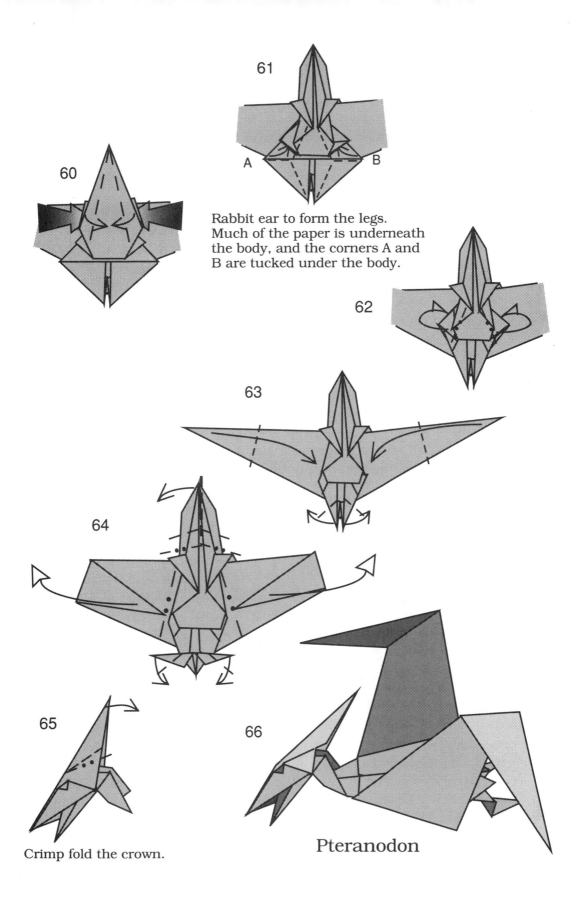

61

60

A   B

Rabbit ear to form the legs.
Much of the paper is underneath
the body, and the corners A and
B are tucked under the body.

62

63

64

65

Crimp fold the crown.

66

Pteranodon

Elasmosaurus

e-LAZ-mo-saw-rus

This marine reptile's name means "ribbon lizard". It was 40 feet long with as many as 76 bones in its neck. Fossils have been found in Kansas which was a shallow sea in the Cretaceous Period. It used its long neck and sharp teeth to dine on fish.

1

Fold and unfold.

2

Kite fold.

7

3

Unfold.

6

If all the lines intersect where the circles are drawn then continue. Otherwise, repeat steps 4-5.

4

Make a guess for this fold, you will find out if it is right in step 6.

5

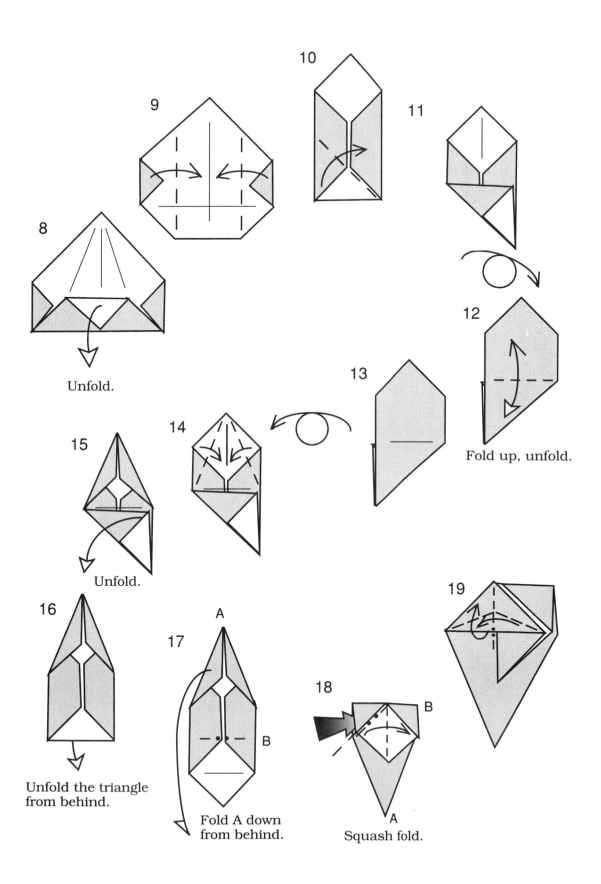

8

9

10

11

Unfold.

12

Fold up, unfold.

13

14

15

Unfold.

16

Unfold the triangle
from behind.

17

A

B

Fold A down
from behind.

18

B

A

Squash fold.

19

ELASMOSAURUS

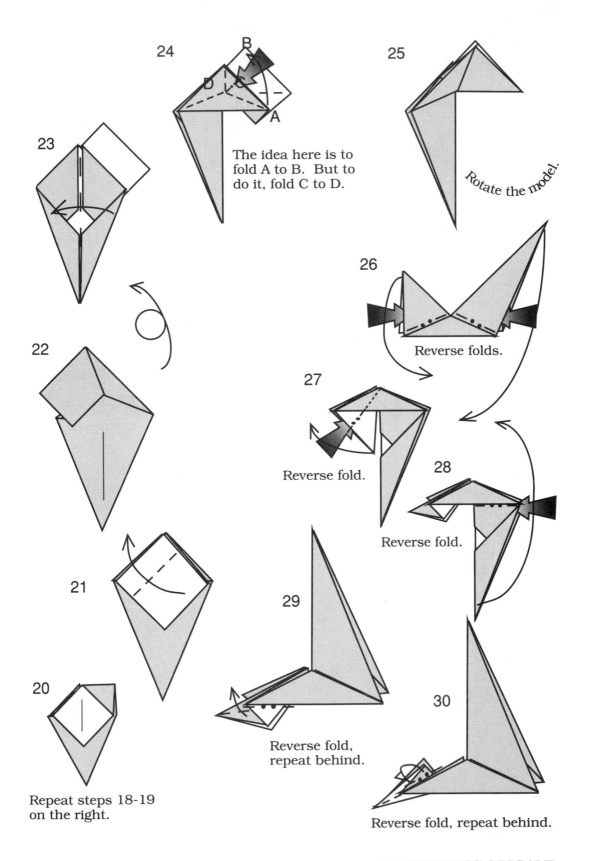

24

B
D C
A

The idea here is to fold A to B. But to do it, fold C to D.

25

Rotate the model.

23

26

Reverse folds.

22

27

Reverse fold.

28

Reverse fold.

21

29

Reverse fold, repeat behind.

20

30

Repeat steps 18-19 on the right.

Reverse fold, repeat behind.

PREHISTORIC ORIGAMI

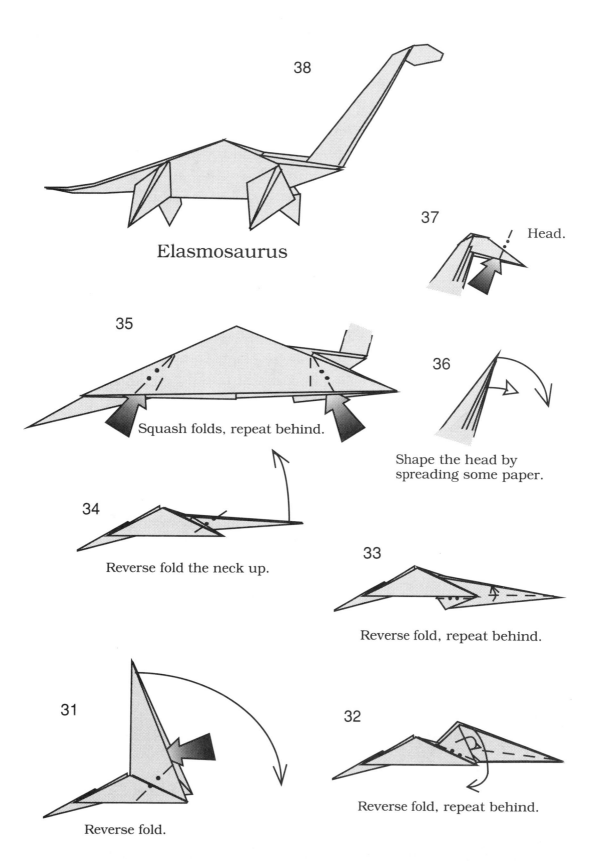

38

Elasmosaurus

37

Head.

35

Squash folds, repeat behind.

36

Shape the head by
spreading some paper.

34

Reverse fold the neck up.

33

Reverse fold, repeat behind.

31

Reverse fold.

32

Reverse fold, repeat behind.

Tanystropheus

tan-e-STRO-fee-us

This lizard lived on the shores of Triassic seas in
Germany. The hip structure clearly prevents it from
being called a dinosaur. Its 9 foot long neck was
more than half its total 15 foot length. It could
remain on the shore and fish for food beneath the
surface of the water.

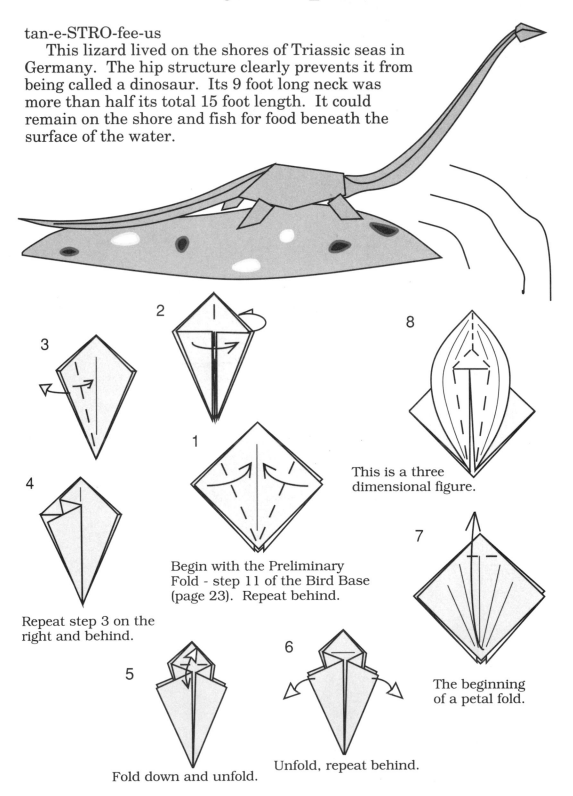

3

2

8

This is a three
dimensional figure.

1

4

Begin with the Preliminary
Fold - step 11 of the Bird Base
(page 23). Repeat behind.

7

Repeat step 3 on the
right and behind.

The beginning
of a petal fold.

5

6

Fold down and unfold.

Unfold, repeat behind.

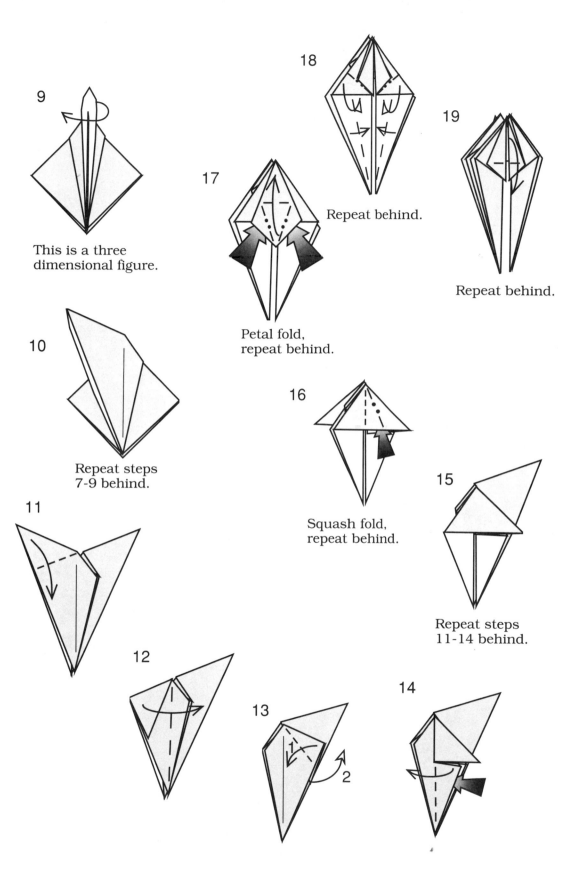

9

This is a three
dimensional figure.

10

Repeat steps
7-9 behind.

11

12

13

2

14

15

Repeat steps
11-14 behind.

16

Squash fold,
repeat behind.

17

Petal fold,
repeat behind.

18

Repeat behind.

19

Repeat behind.

TANYSTROPHEUS

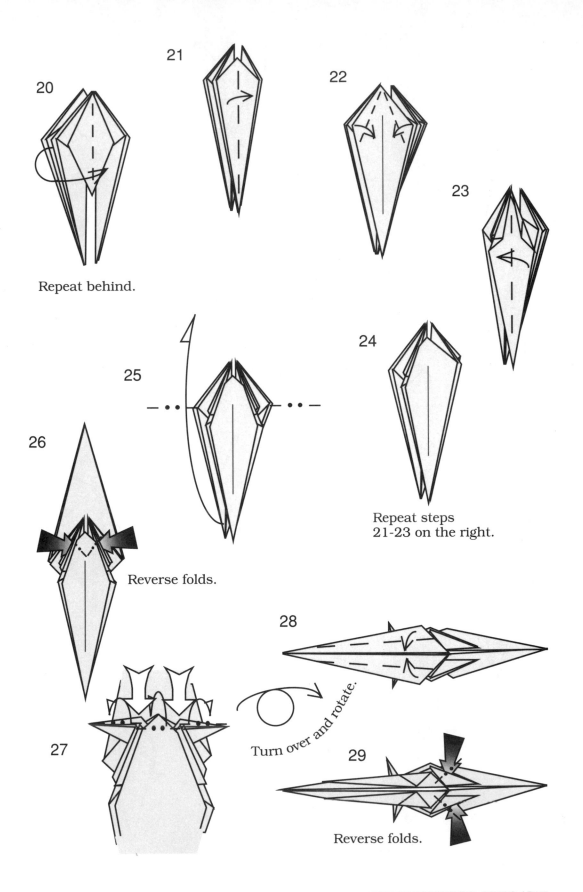

20

21

22

23

Repeat behind.

24

25

26

Repeat steps
21-23 on the right.

Reverse folds.

28

Turn over and rotate.

27

29

Reverse folds.

PREHISTORIC ORIGAMI

37

Tanystropheus

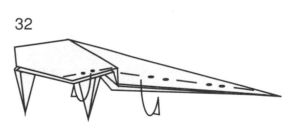

36

Head.

34

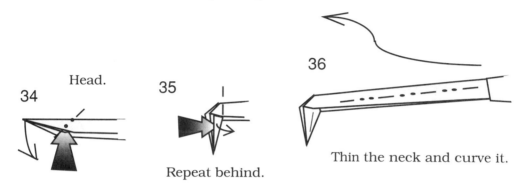

35

Repeat behind.

Thin the neck and curve it.

33

Squash folds. Repeat behind.

32

Repeat behind.

31

30

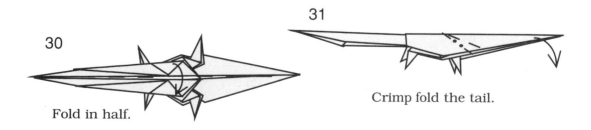

Crimp fold the tail.

Fold in half.

Apatosaurus

a-PAT-oh-saw-rus

    This dinosaur is better known as Brontosaurus, the "thunder lizard" but more correctly named Apatosaurus, the "headless lizard". It was 70 feet long and very heavy. The front legs were shorter than the back legs. Its fossils were found in the western U.S. with other Jurassic dinosaurs. Its small flat teeth could not have ground up all the food required to fuel this animal so it relied on "gizzard stones" to aid in digestion.

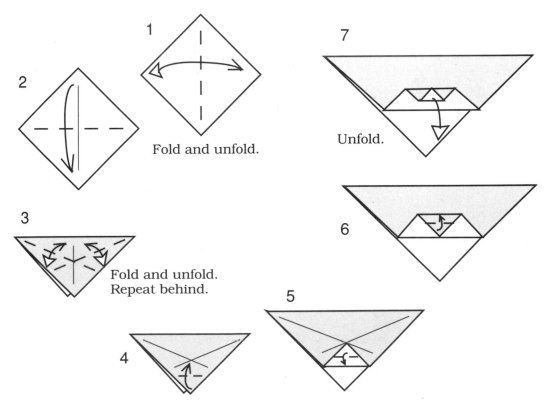

1

Fold and unfold.

2

3

Fold and unfold.
Repeat behind.

4

5

6

7

Unfold.

12

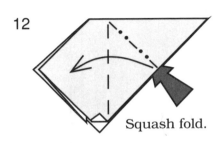

Squash fold.

13

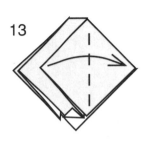

11

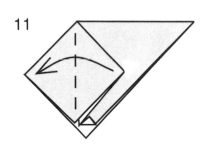

14

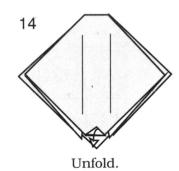

Unfold.

10

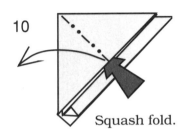

Squash fold.

15

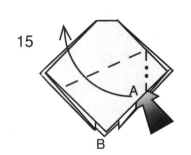

Squash fold. The valley fold
line is on an existing crease.

9

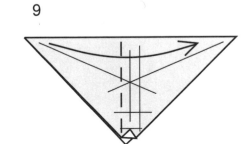

16

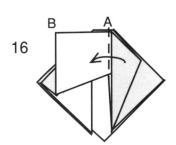

8

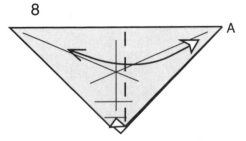

Fold A to the left, then unfold.

17

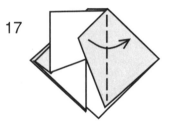

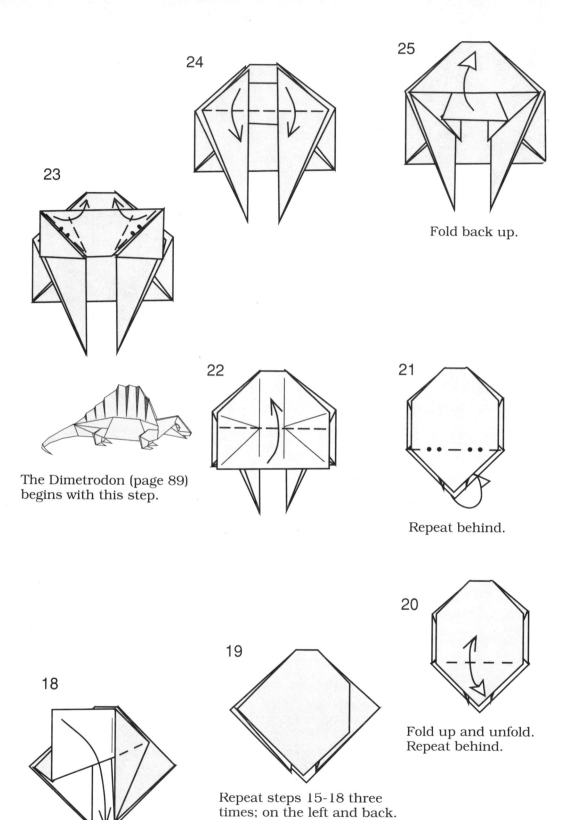

24

25

Fold back up.

23

22

The Dimetrodon (page 89) begins with this step.

21

Repeat behind.

20

Fold up and unfold.
Repeat behind.

19

Repeat steps 15-18 three times; on the left and back.

18

PREHISTORIC ORIGAMI

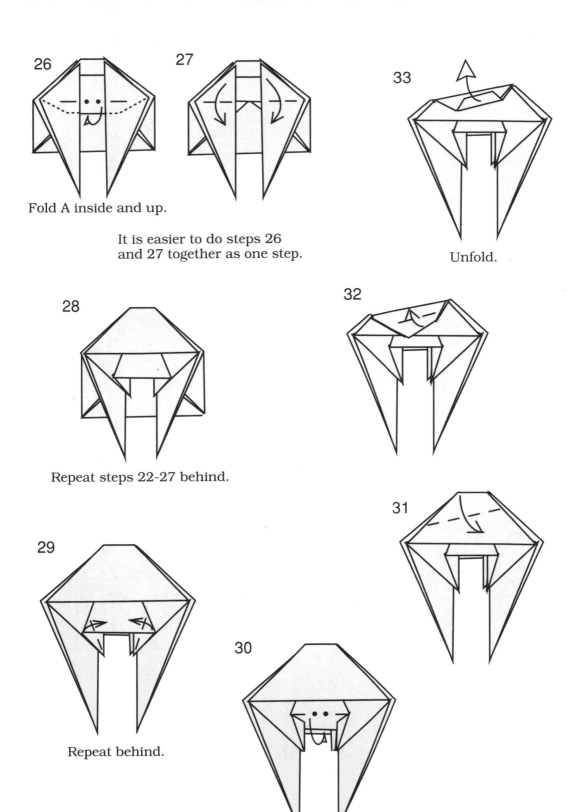

26

Fold A inside and up.

It is easier to do steps 26
and 27 together as one step.

27

33

Unfold.

28

Repeat steps 22-27 behind.

32

29

Repeat behind.

30

Repeat behind.

31

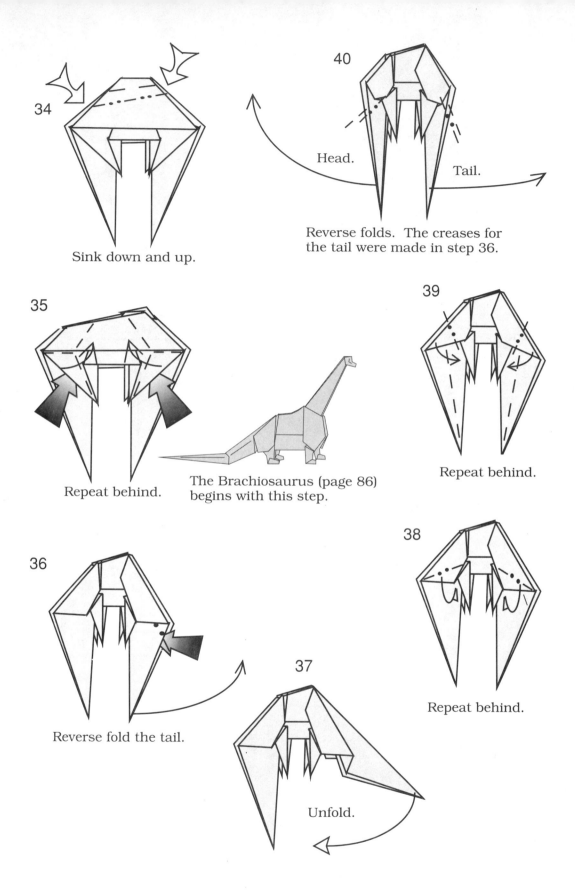

34 Sink down and up.

40 Head. Tail.
Reverse folds. The creases for the tail were made in step 36.

35 Repeat behind.

The Brachiosaurus (page 86) begins with this step.

39 Repeat behind.

36 Reverse fold the tail.

37 Unfold.

38 Repeat behind.

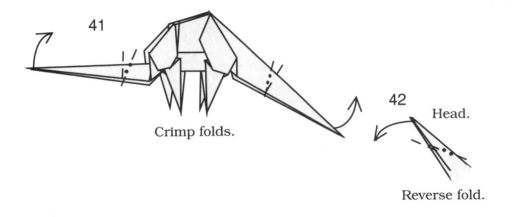

41

Crimp folds.

42

Head.

Reverse fold.

43

Spread the head while it is folded down.

44

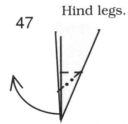

Reverse fold.

45

Front legs.

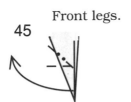

Repeat behind.

46

Repeat behind.

47

Hind legs.

Repeat behind.

48

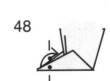

Repeat behind.

49

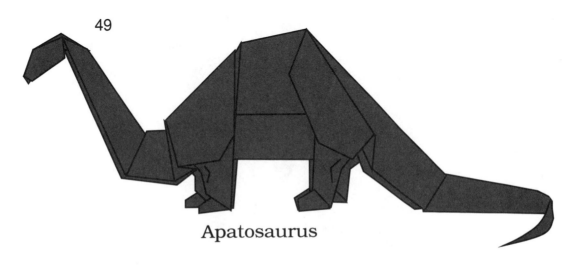

Apatosaurus

Brachiosaurus

BRAKE-ee-oh-saw-rus

This 75 foot long, Jurassic dinosaur was called "arm lizard" because its front legs were longer than its back legs. The placement of the nose on top of its head was once thought to aid in breathing when submerged in deep water. Now some paleontologists believe it lived on high ground, eating pine needles, since the skeleton could not have withstood the pressure of deep water. Fossils were found in Colorado.

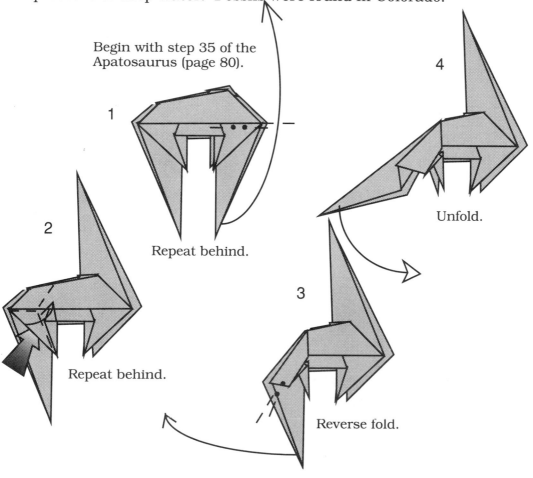

Begin with step 35 of the Apatosaurus (page 80).

1

Repeat behind.

2

Repeat behind.

3

Reverse fold.

4

Unfold.

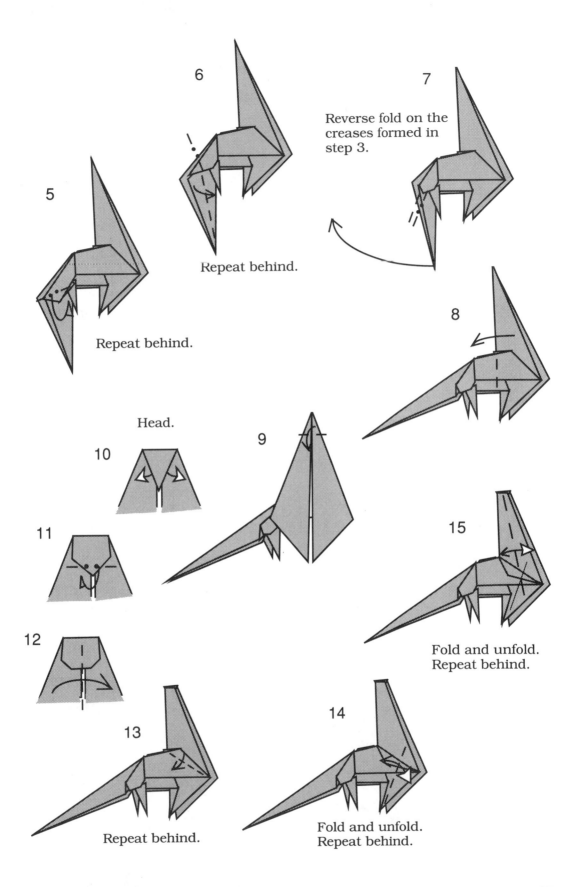

5

Repeat behind.

6

Repeat behind.

7

Reverse fold on the creases formed in step 3.

8

9

Head.

10

11

12

13

Repeat behind.

14

Fold and unfold.
Repeat behind.

15

Fold and unfold.
Repeat behind.

BRACHIOSAURUS

87

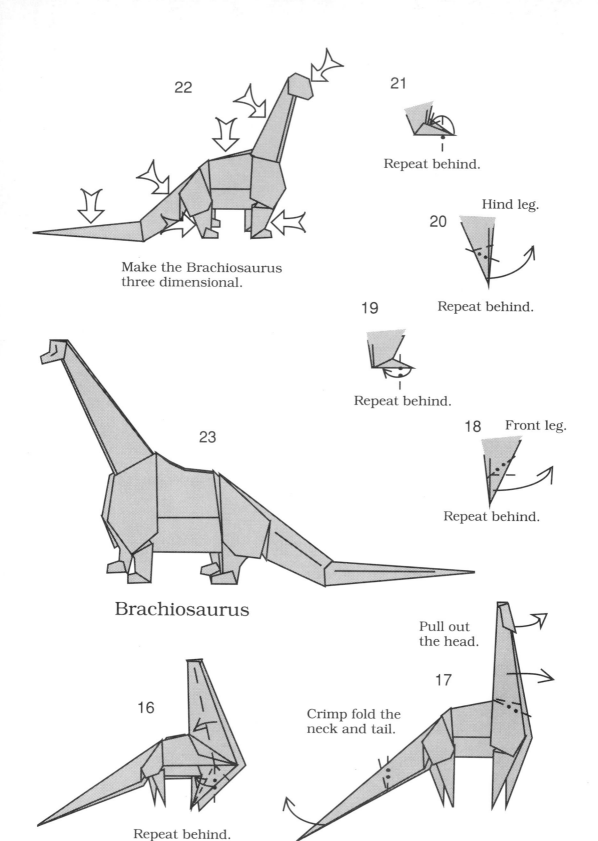

22

Make the Brachiosaurus
three dimensional.

21

Repeat behind.

Hind leg.

20

Repeat behind.

19

Repeat behind.

18 Front leg.

Repeat behind.

23

Brachiosaurus

16

Repeat behind.

Pull out
the head.

17

Crimp fold the
neck and tail.

PREHISTORIC ORIGAMI

Dimetrodon

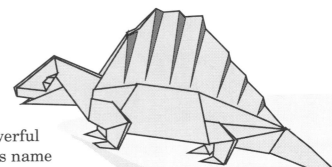

di-ME-tro-don

    This was a very powerful meat eating reptile. Its name means "double measure tooth" because of its many knife-like teeth. It lived in the Permian Period immediately preceding the Mesozoic Era. It was about 10 feet long and the "sail" on its back helped regulate its body temperature.

1

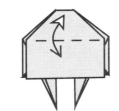

Begin with step 22 of the Apatosaurus (page 80).

Fold down, then unfold.

2

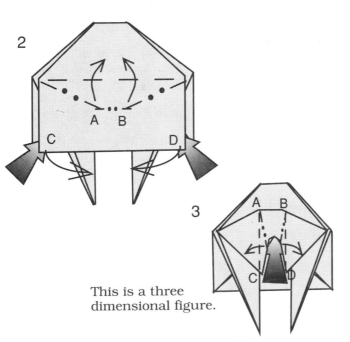

3

This is a three dimensional figure.

5

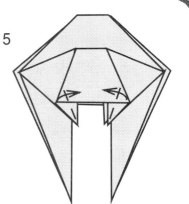

Repeat behind.

4

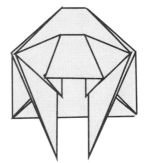

Repeat steps 1-3 behind.

6

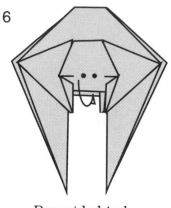

Repeat behind.

11

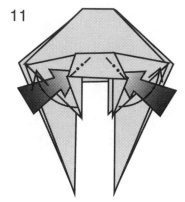

Reverse folds, repeat behind.

7

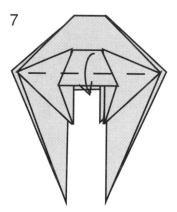

Repeat behind.

10

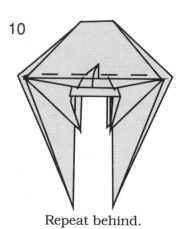

Repeat behind.

8

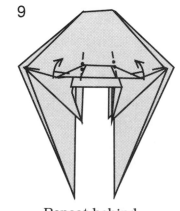

Repeat behind.

9

Repeat behind.

PREHISTORIC ORIGAMI

12

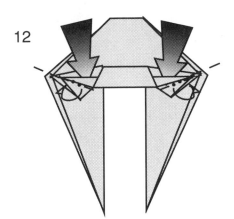

Reverse folds, repeat behind.

13

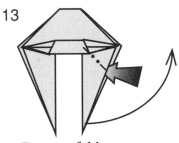

Reverse fold.

14

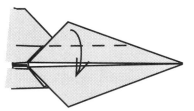

Tail.

15

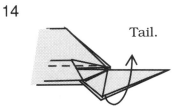

16

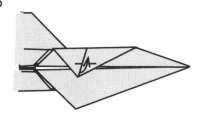

Head.

21

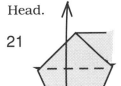

22

20

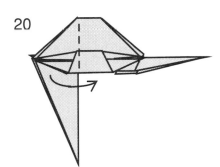

19

18

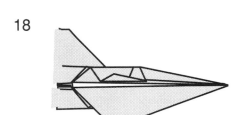

Repeat steps 15-17 on
the lower part of the tail.

17

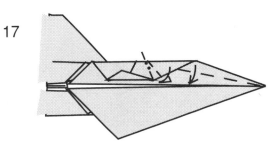

23

24

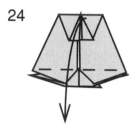

25

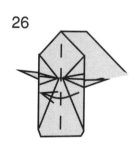

26

27

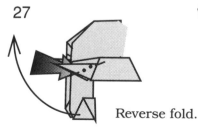

Reverse fold.

28

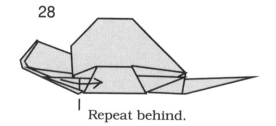

Repeat behind.

29

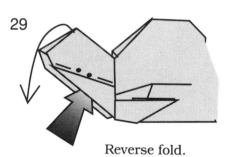

Reverse fold.

30

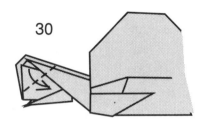

Repeat behind.

31

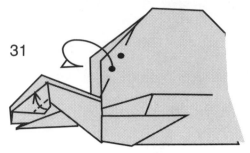

Form the eye. Repeat behind.

PREHISTORIC ORIGAMI

32

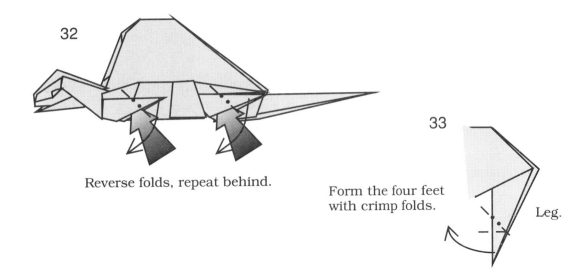

Reverse folds, repeat behind.

33

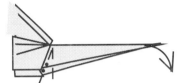

Form the four feet
with crimp folds.

Leg.

34

Crimp fold the tail so the
tip will be lower than the
body, then curl it.

35

Pleat Dimetrodon's sail.

36

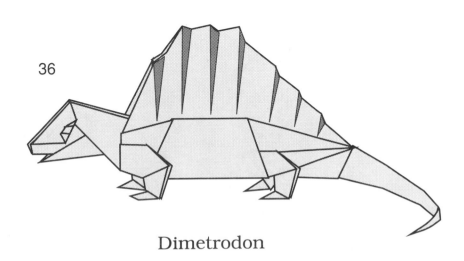

Dimetrodon

Spinosaurus

SPINE-oh-saw-rus

This 40 foot long dinosaur was a fierce meat eater. The sail down its back helped control its body heat. Fossils were found in Egypt. It lived at the end of the Cretaceous Period. Spinosaurus means "spine lizard". Despite the sail, Spinosaurus was not related to Dimetrodon.

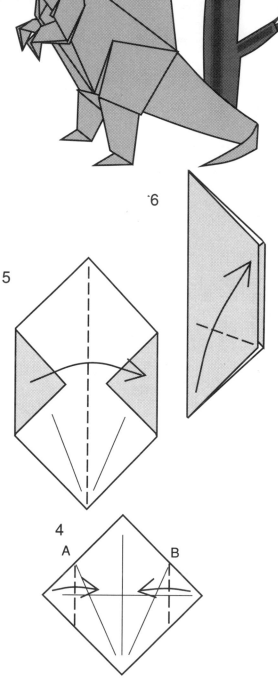

1

Fold and unfold.

2

3

Unfold.

4

A   B

Use points A and B as guides.

5

6

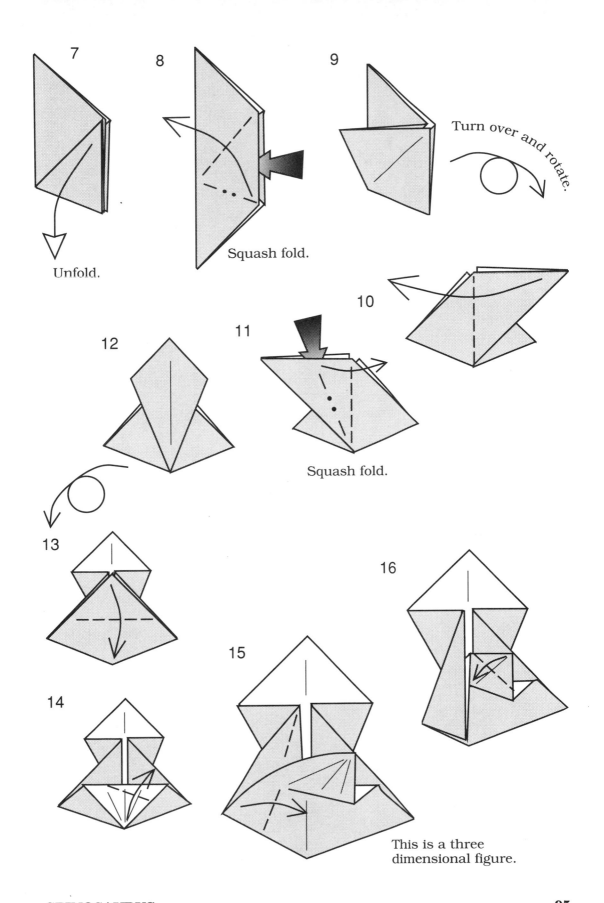

7

8

Squash fold.

9

Turn over and rotate.

10

11

Squash fold.

12

13

14

15

This is a three
dimensional figure.

16

Unfold.

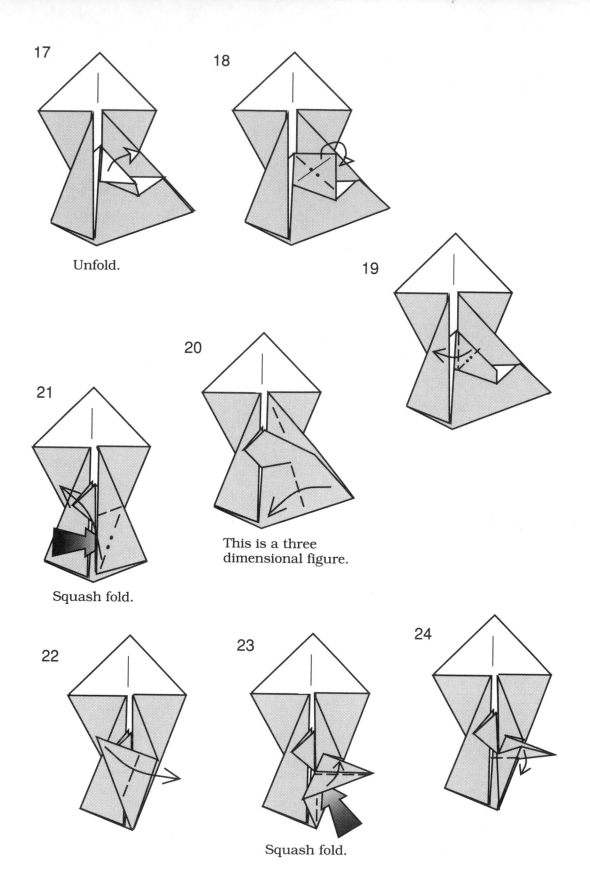

17

18

Unfold.

19

20

This is a three
dimensional figure.

21

Squash fold.

22

23

Squash fold.

24

PREHISTORIC ORIGAMI

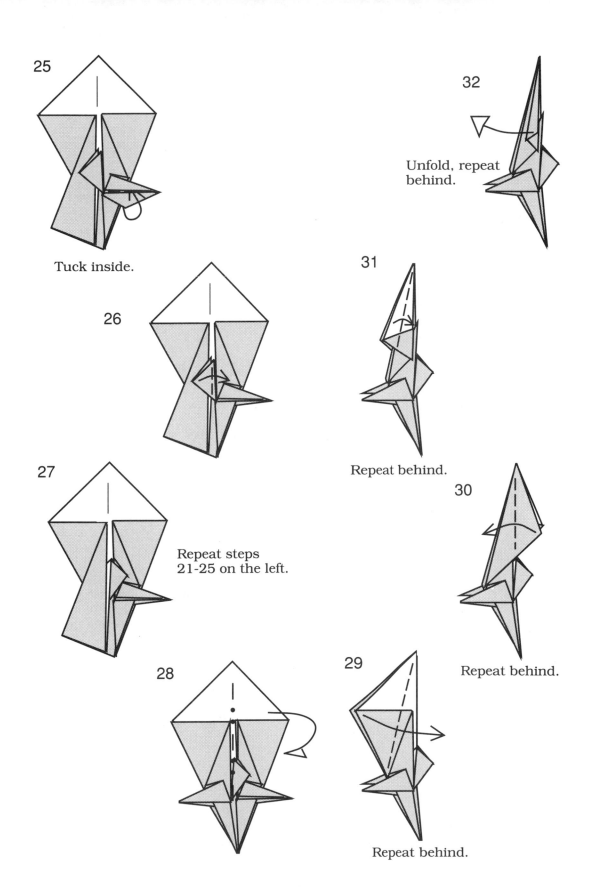

25

Tuck inside.

26

27

Repeat steps
21-25 on the left.

28

29

Repeat behind.

30

Repeat behind.

31

Repeat behind.

32

Unfold, repeat
behind.

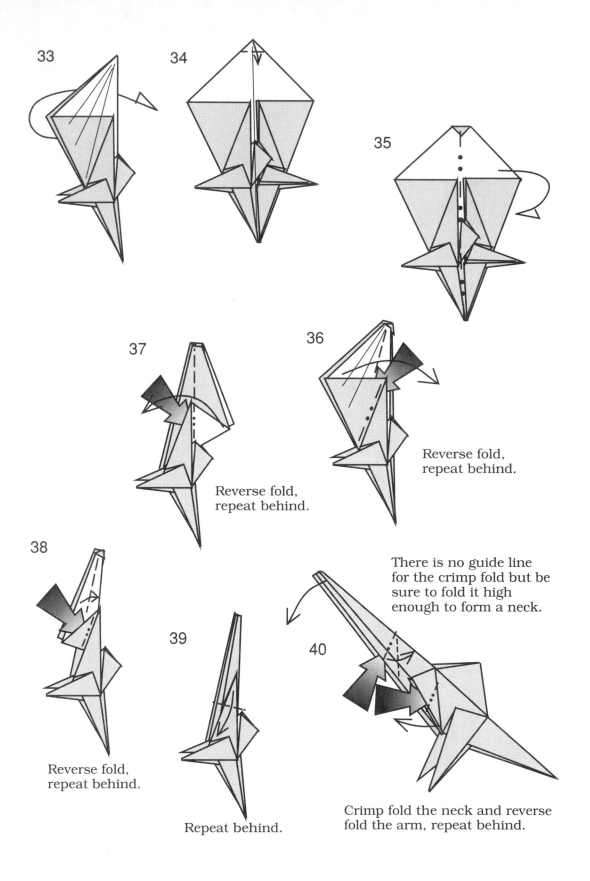

33

34

35

37

Reverse fold,
repeat behind.

36

Reverse fold,
repeat behind.

38

Reverse fold,
repeat behind.

39

Repeat behind.

There is no guide line
for the crimp fold but be
sure to fold it high
enough to form a neck.

40

Crimp fold the neck and reverse
fold the arm, repeat behind.

PREHISTORIC ORIGAMI

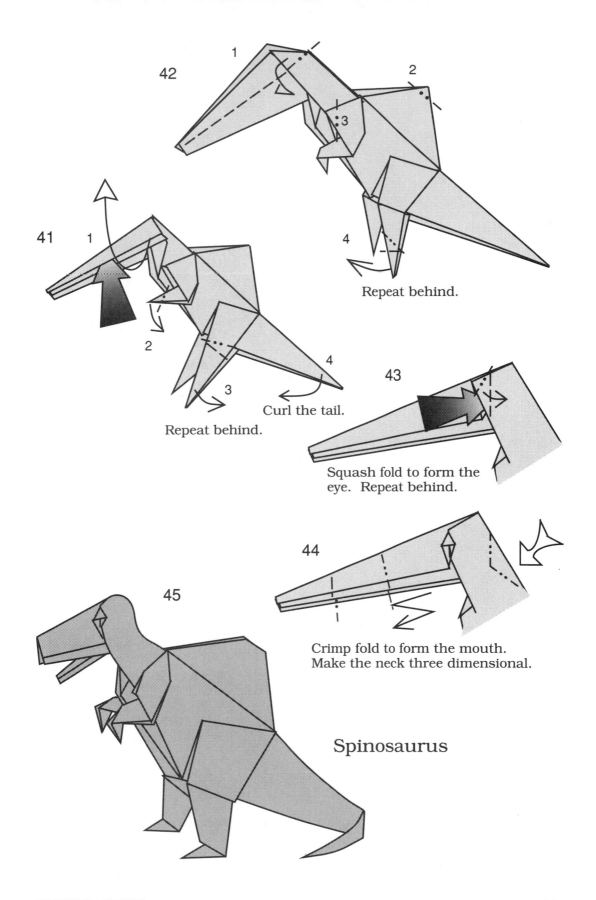

42

41

1

2

3

4

Repeat behind.

2

3

4

Curl the tail.

Repeat behind.

43

Squash fold to form the
eye. Repeat behind.

44

Crimp fold to form the mouth.
Make the neck three dimensional.

45

Spinosaurus

Tyrannosaurus

ti-RAN-oh-saw-rus

Probably the largest meat eater ever to walk the earth, this "tyrant lizard" was up to 50 feet long. The 6 inch dagger-like teeth were perfect for eating other Cretaceous animals. Once thought to be feared, some paleontologists now believe it was a scavenger, and could be easily beaten in a fight. Its arms were so small and weak that it probably could not get up if knocked over by the swing of a heavy tail. It used its claws like knives but could not reach its hand to its mouth.

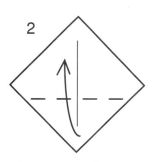

2

Make a guess for this first fold. In step 4 you will find out if you were correct.

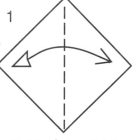

1

Fold and unfold.

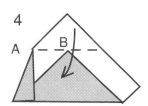

4

3

A   B

If A and B lie on the same horizontal line, then continue. Otherwise, try a better guess in step 2.

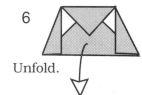

6

Unfold.

5

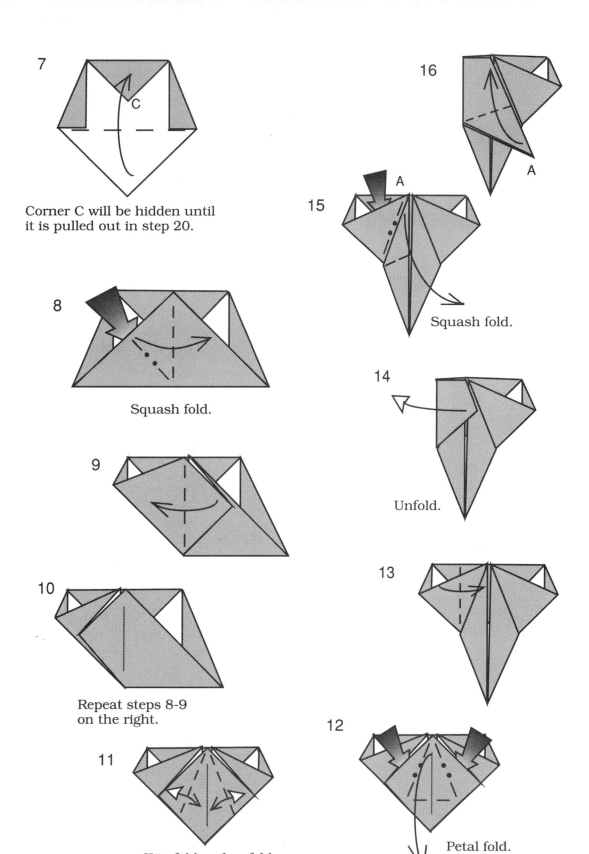

7

Corner C will be hidden until it is pulled out in step 20.

8

Squash fold.

9

10

Repeat steps 8-9 on the right.

11

Kite fold and unfold.

12

Petal fold.

13

14

Unfold.

15

Squash fold.

16

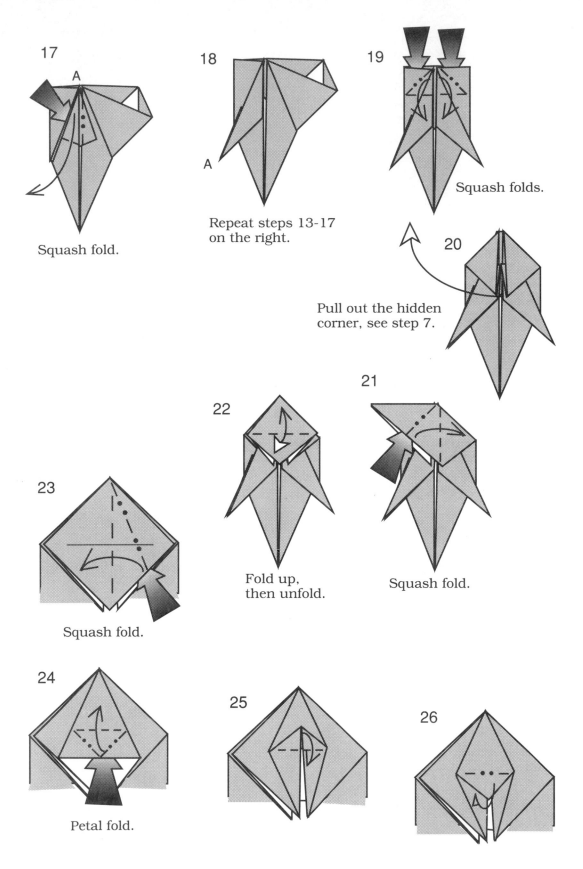

17

A

Squash fold.

18

A

Repeat steps 13-17
on the right.

19

Squash folds.

20

Pull out the hidden
corner, see step 7.

21

Squash fold.

22

Fold up,
then unfold.

23

Squash fold.

24

Petal fold.

25

26

31

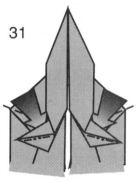

Reverse folds.

32

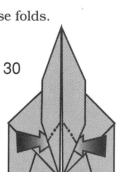

33

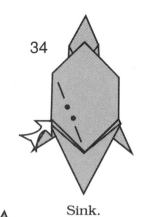

Fold and unfold.

30

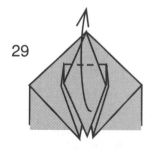

Reverse folds.

34

Sink.

29

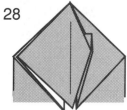

35

Note that the folds do not come to a point at the top.

28

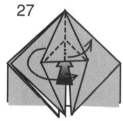

Repeat steps 23-27 on the left side.

36

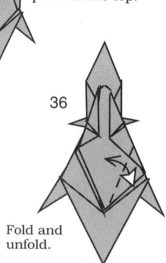

Fold and unfold.

27

TYRANNOSAURUS

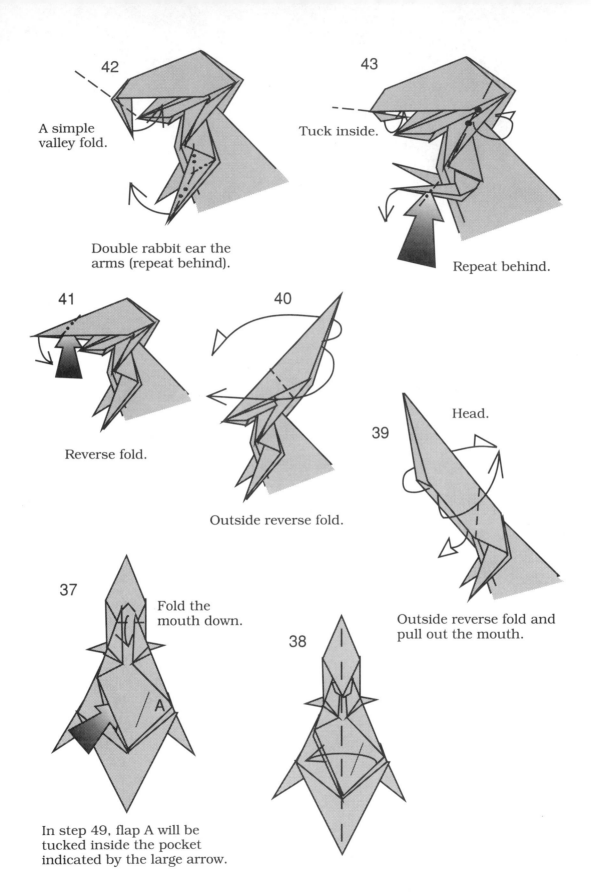

42

A simple
valley fold.

Double rabbit ear the
arms (repeat behind).

43

Tuck inside.

Repeat behind.

41

Reverse fold.

40

Outside reverse fold.

39

Head.

Outside reverse fold and
pull out the mouth.

37

Fold the
mouth down.

A

38

In step 49, flap A will be
tucked inside the pocket
indicated by the large arrow.

PREHISTORIC ORIGAMI

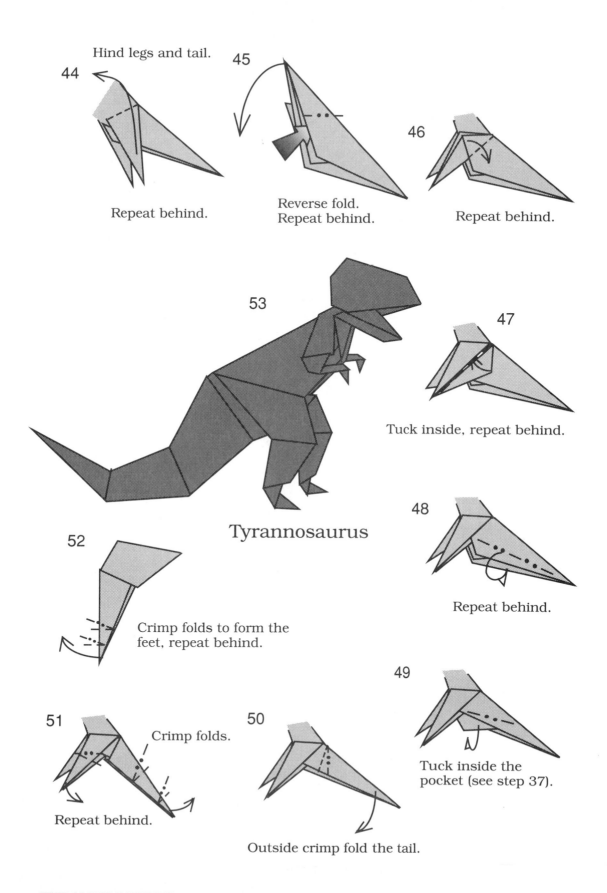

Hind legs and tail.

44

45

Repeat behind.

Reverse fold.
Repeat behind.

46

Repeat behind.

53

47

Tuck inside, repeat behind.

Tyrannosaurus

48

Repeat behind.

52

Crimp folds to form the
feet, repeat behind.

49

Tuck inside the
pocket (see step 37).

51

Crimp folds.

50

Repeat behind.

Outside crimp fold the tail.

Hadrosaurus

had-ro-SAW-rus

Formerly known as Trachodon, the "rough tooth", this duck billed dinosaur was 33 feet long. Behind the bill were 2000 teeth used for grinding water plants. Hadrosaurus means "bulky lizard" and was the first dinosaur skeleton ever excavated in the U.S. It was found in New Jersey in 1858. Mummified skin has also been found of this Cretaceous creature.

1

Fold and unfold.

2

Fold and unfold.

3

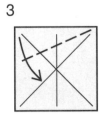

4

5

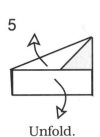

Unfold.

6

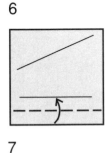

7

8

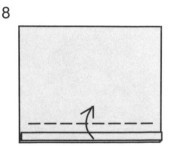

Fold up on the existing crease.

9

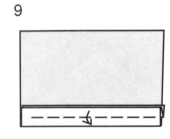

106

PREHISTORIC ORIGAMI

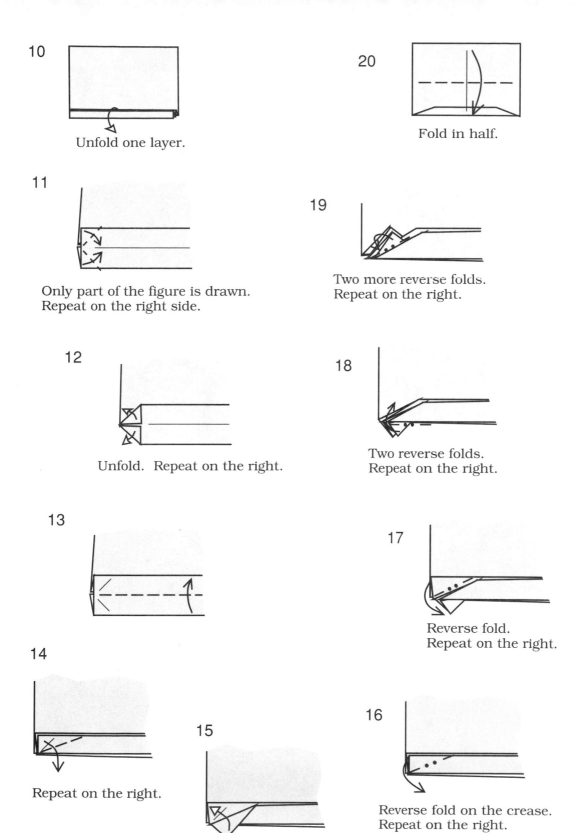

10

Unfold one layer.

20

Fold in half.

11

Only part of the figure is drawn.
Repeat on the right side.

19

Two more reverse folds.
Repeat on the right.

12

Unfold. Repeat on the right.

18

Two reverse folds.
Repeat on the right.

13

17

Reverse fold.
Repeat on the right.

14

Repeat on the right.

15

Unfold. Repeat on the right.

16

Reverse fold on the crease.
Repeat on the right.

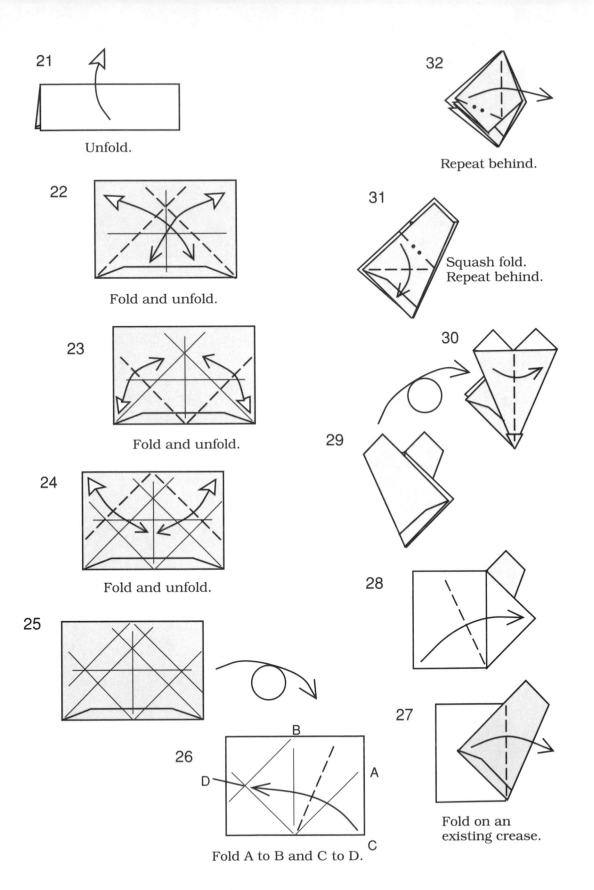

21 Unfold.

22 Fold and unfold.

23 Fold and unfold.

24 Fold and unfold.

25

26 Fold A to B and C to D.

27 Fold on an existing crease.

28

29

30

31 Squash fold. Repeat behind.

32 Repeat behind.

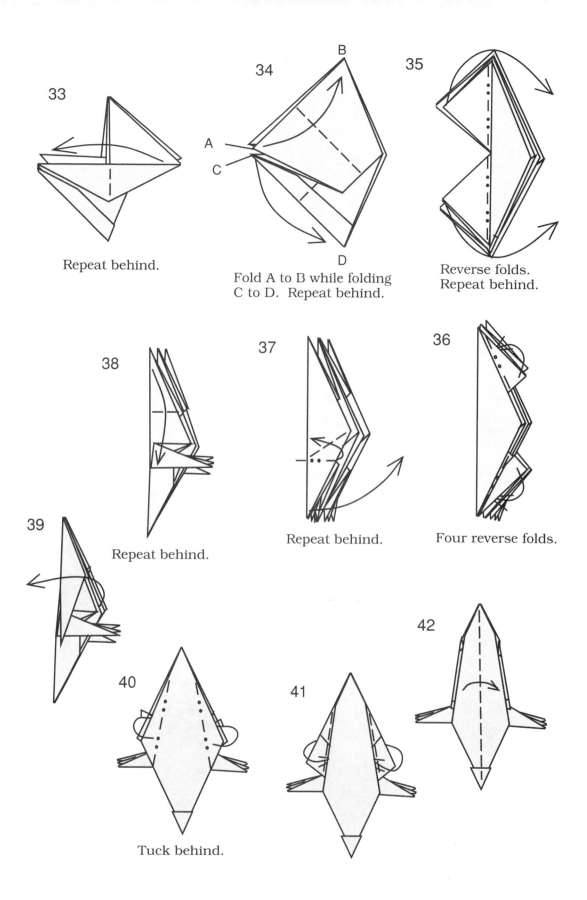

33

Repeat behind.

34

A
C
B
D

Fold A to B while folding
C to D. Repeat behind.

35

Reverse folds.
Repeat behind.

38

Repeat behind.

37

Repeat behind.

36

Four reverse folds.

39

40

Tuck behind.

41

42

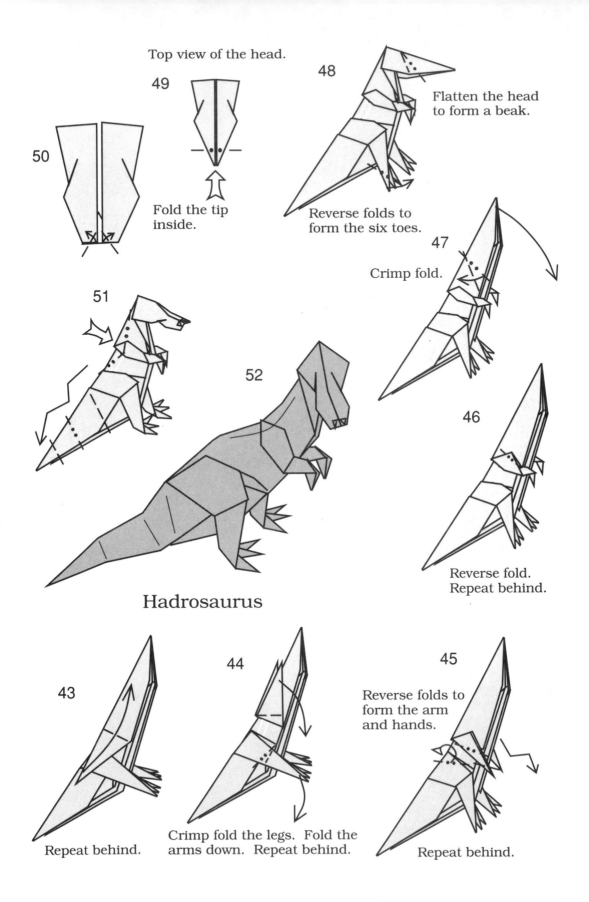

Top view of the head.

49

50

Fold the tip
inside.

48

Flatten the head
to form a beak.

Reverse folds to
form the six toes.

47

Crimp fold.

51

52

46

Reverse fold.
Repeat behind.

Hadrosaurus

43

44

45

Repeat behind.

Crimp fold the legs. Fold the
arms down. Repeat behind.

Reverse folds to
form the arm
and hands.

Repeat behind.

Iguanodon

i-GWA-no-don

The most distinguishing feature of this Cretaceous dinosaur is the spike-like thumbs on its front legs. Standing on its hind legs, this reptile stood 16 feet tall. However, it could have also walked on four legs. It had grinding teeth in the back of its mouth and a strong beak with which to break off plants. One of the first dinosaurs ever discovered, fossils were found in Belguim and North Africa. Iguanodon means "iguana tooth".

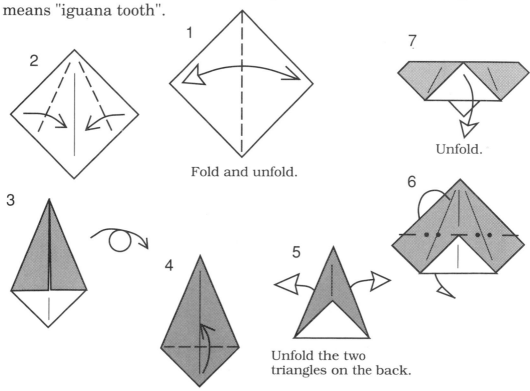

1

Fold and unfold.

2

3

4

5

Unfold the two triangles on the back.

6

7

Unfold.

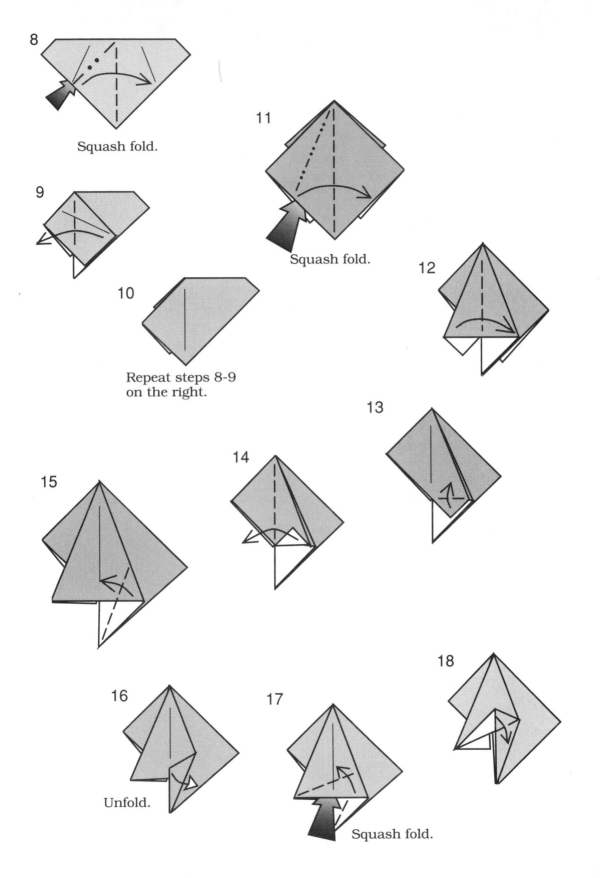

8

Squash fold.

9

10

Repeat steps 8-9
on the right.

11

Squash fold.

12

13

14

15

16

Unfold.

17

Squash fold.

18

PREHISTORIC ORIGAMI

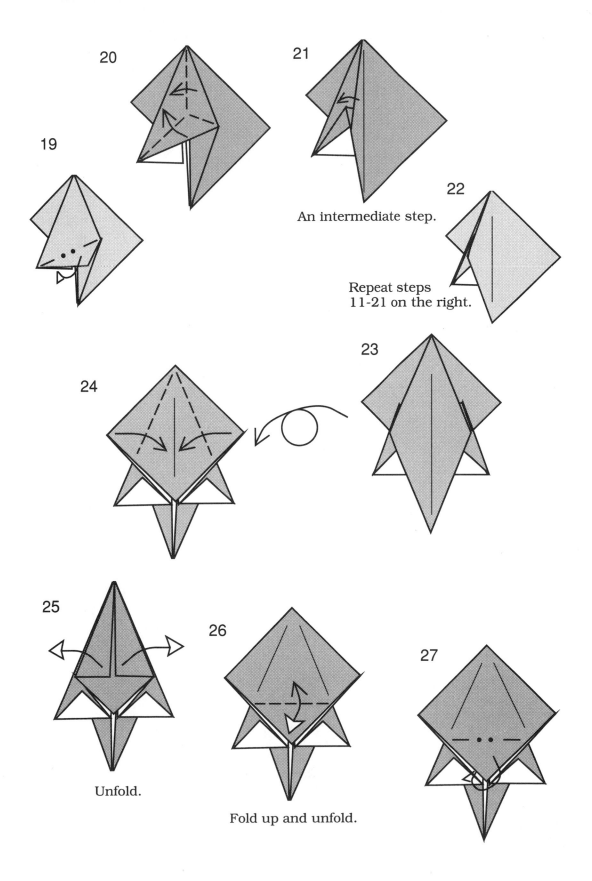

19

20

21

An intermediate step.

22

Repeat steps
11-21 on the right.

23

24

25

Unfold.

26

Fold up and unfold.

27

IGUANODON

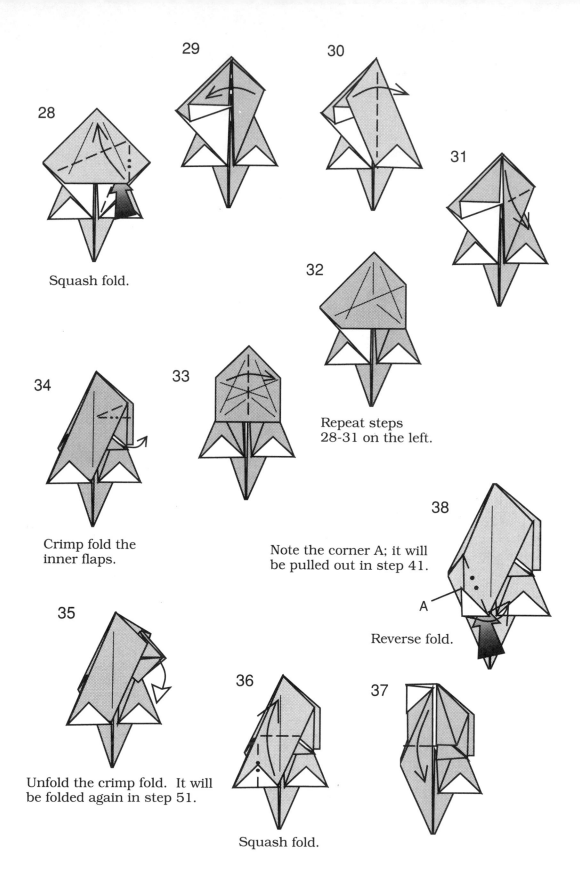

28

Squash fold.

29

30

31

32

Repeat steps
28-31 on the left.

34

Crimp fold the
inner flaps.

33

38

Note the corner A; it will
be pulled out in step 41.

A

Reverse fold.

35

Unfold the crimp fold. It will
be folded again in step 51.

36

Squash fold.

37

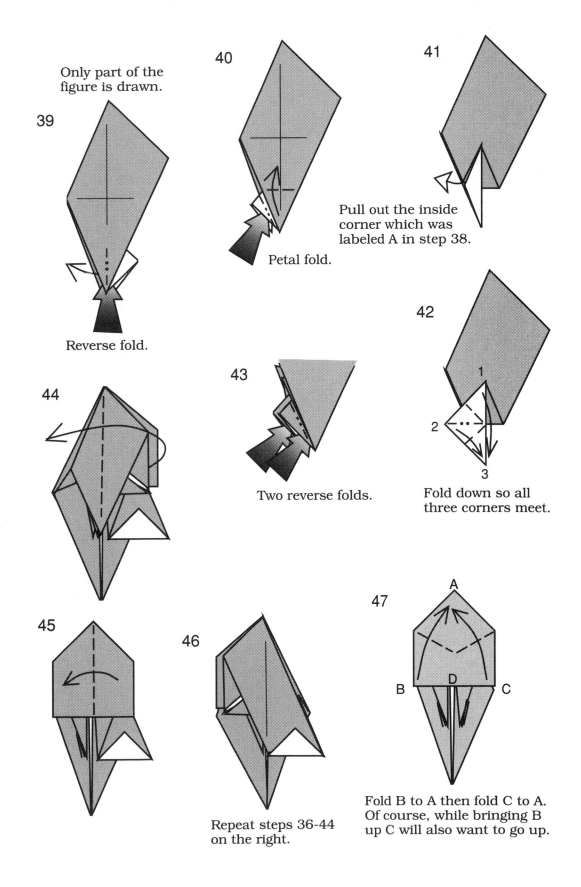

39

Only part of the figure is drawn.

Reverse fold.

40

Petal fold.

41

Pull out the inside corner which was labeled A in step 38.

42

Fold down so all three corners meet.

43

Two reverse folds.

44

45

46

Repeat steps 36-44 on the right.

47

Fold B to A then fold C to A. Of course, while bringing B up C will also want to go up.

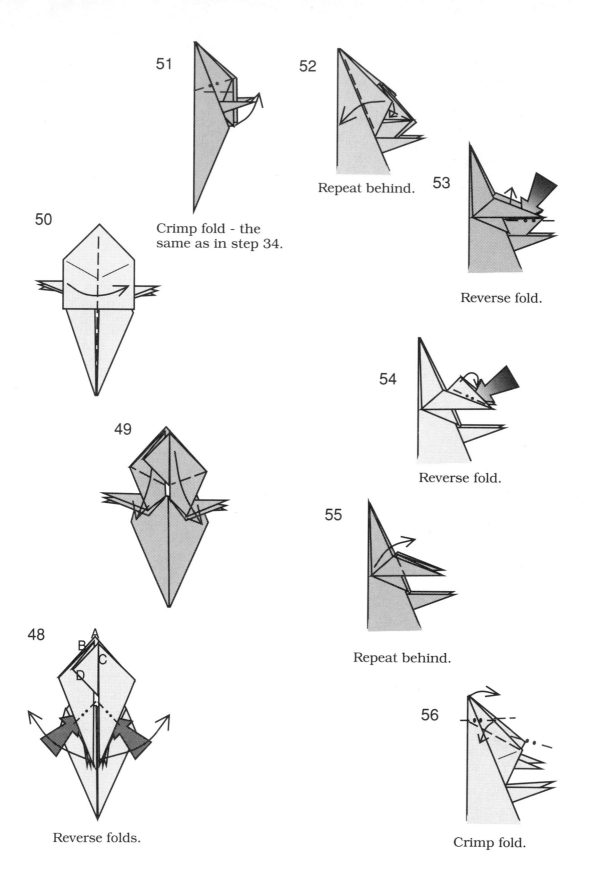

51

52

Repeat behind.

53

Reverse fold.

50

Crimp fold - the
same as in step 34.

54

Reverse fold.

49

55

Repeat behind.

48

56

Reverse folds.

Crimp fold.

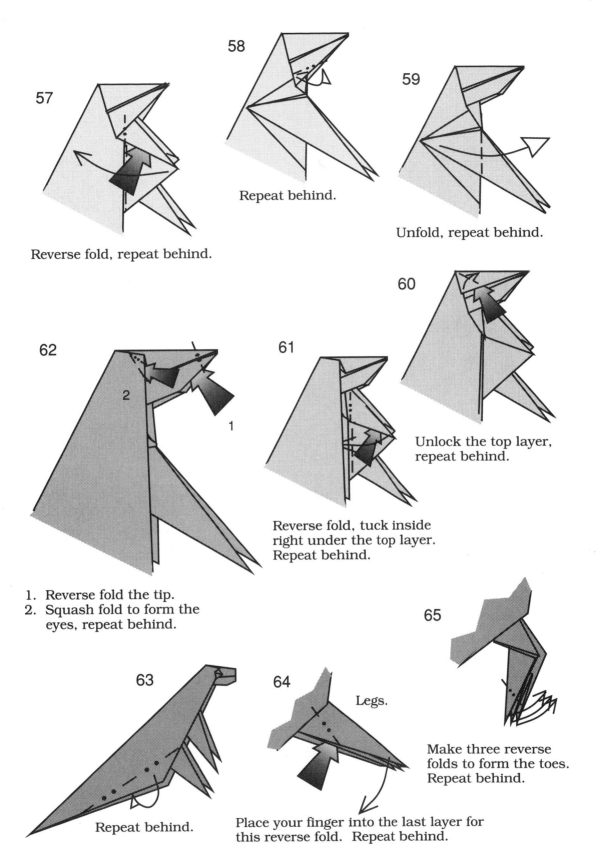

57

Reverse fold, repeat behind.

58

Repeat behind.

59

Unfold, repeat behind.

60

61

Unlock the top layer, repeat behind.

Reverse fold, tuck inside right under the top layer. Repeat behind.

62

2

1

1. Reverse fold the tip.
2. Squash fold to form the eyes, repeat behind.

63

Repeat behind.

64

Legs.

Place your finger into the last layer for this reverse fold. Repeat behind.

65

Make three reverse folds to form the toes. Repeat behind.

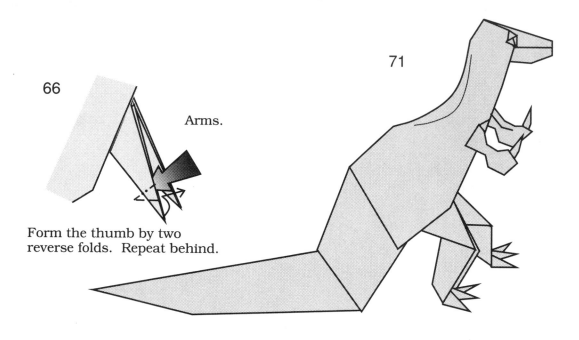

66

Arms.

Form the thumb by two
reverse folds. Repeat behind.

71

Iguanodon

67

Repeat behind.

70

Tail.

Shape the tail with crimp folds.

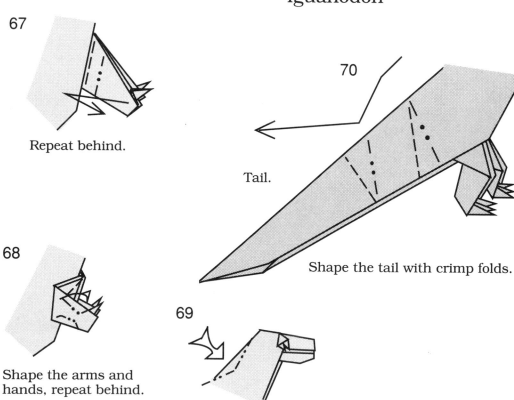

68

Shape the arms and
hands, repeat behind.

69

Make the neck
three dimensional.

Protoceratops

pro-toe-SER-a-tops

The "first horn face" fossils were discovered in Mongolia and showed paleontologists how dinosaurs may have cared for their young. The nests included unhatched eggs as well as skeletons of babies. The adults grew to 6 feet long. These were Cretaceous plant eaters with parrot like beaks and bone covered faces.

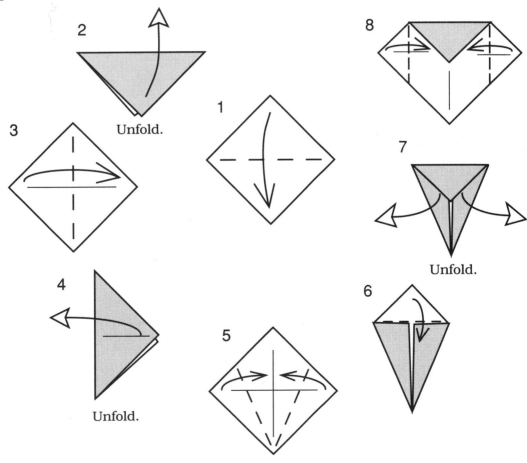

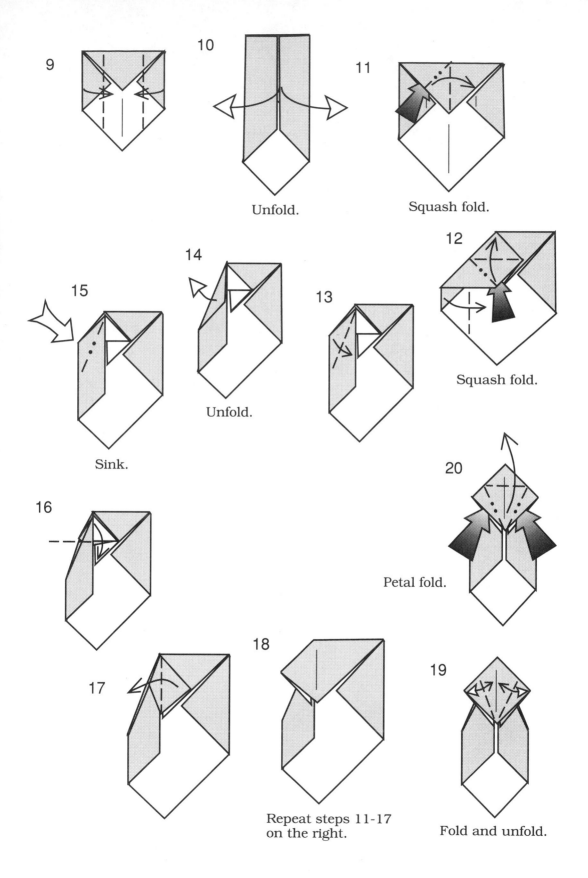

9

10

Unfold.

11

Squash fold.

14

Unfold.

15

Sink.

13

12

Squash fold.

16

20

Petal fold.

17

18

Repeat steps 11-17
on the right.

19

Fold and unfold.

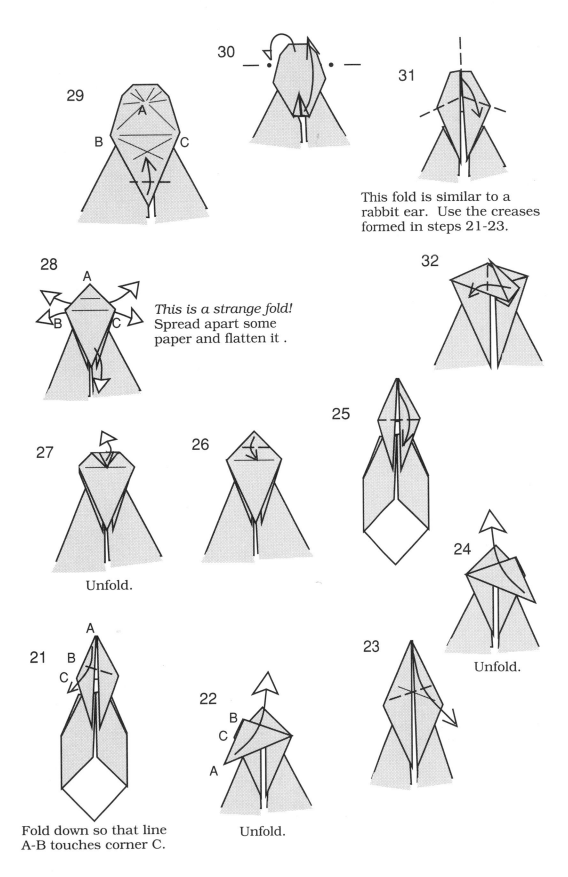

29

A

B   C

30

31

This fold is similar to a
rabbit ear. Use the creases
formed in steps 21-23.

28

A

B   C

This is a strange fold!
Spread apart some
paper and flatten it .

32

25

27

Unfold.

26

24

Unfold.

23

21

A
B
C

Fold down so that line
A-B touches corner C.

22

B
C
A

Unfold.

33

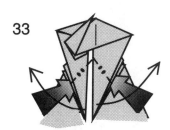

Reverse folds.

34

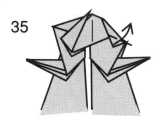

There are no guide lines for this fold.

35

36

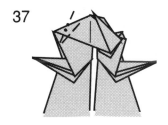

37

Repeat steps 34-35 on the left.

43

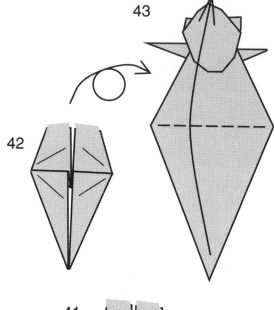

42

41

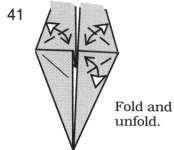

Fold and unfold.

40

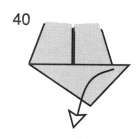

Unfold.

39

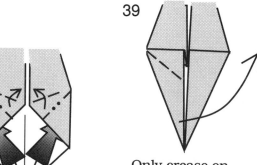

Only crease on half of the line.

38

PREHISTORIC ORIGAMI

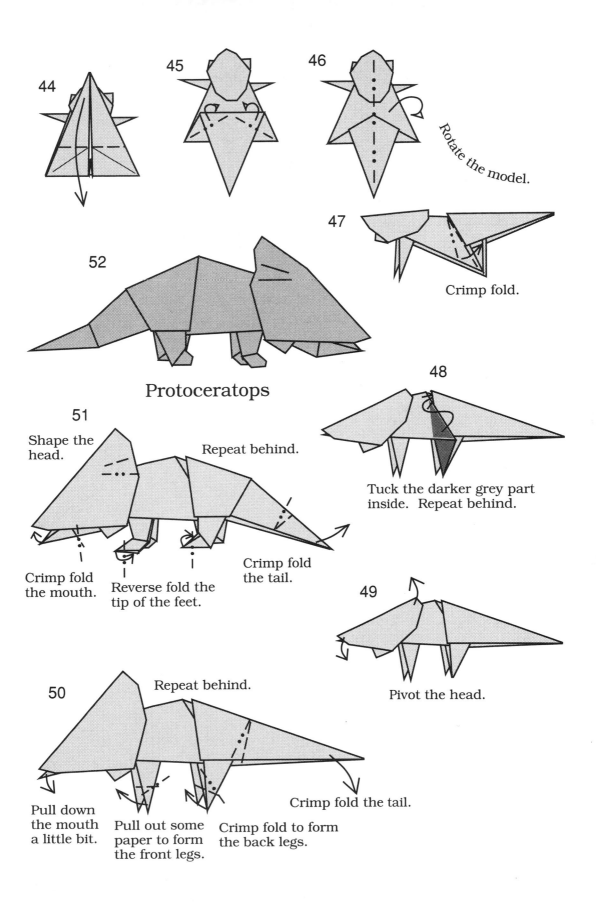

44

45

46

Rotate the model.

47

Crimp fold.

52

Protoceratops

48

Tuck the darker grey part inside. Repeat behind.

51

Shape the head.

Repeat behind.

Crimp fold the mouth.

Reverse fold the tip of the feet.

Crimp fold the tail.

49

Pivot the head.

50

Repeat behind.

Pull down the mouth a little bit.

Pull out some paper to form the front legs.

Crimp fold to form the back legs.

Crimp fold the tail.

Triceratops

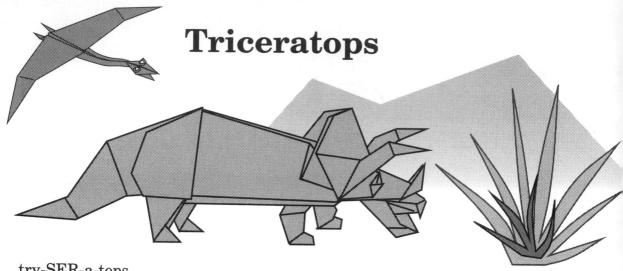

try-SER-a-tops

A peaceful plant eater, Triceratops was 30 feet long. It had a beak like a parrot. Its name means "three horn face" and the horns over its eyes were 3 feet long. The tough, leathery skin and the bony frill protecting its neck made Triceratops one of the best protected dinosaurs. It is thought to be the last one to succumb to extinction at the end of the Cretaceous.

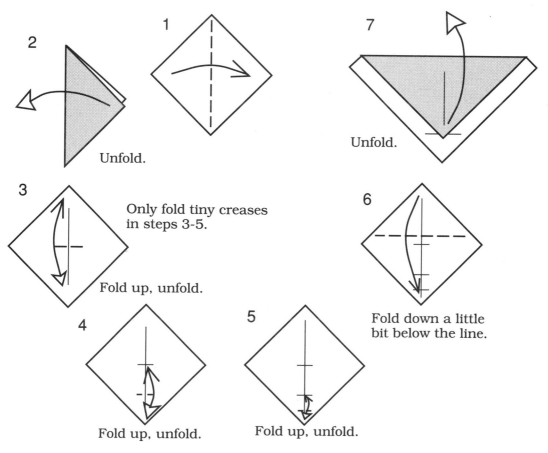

1

2

Unfold.

3

Only fold tiny creases in steps 3-5.

Fold up, unfold.

4

Fold up, unfold.

5

Fold up, unfold.

6

Fold down a little bit below the line.

7

Unfold.

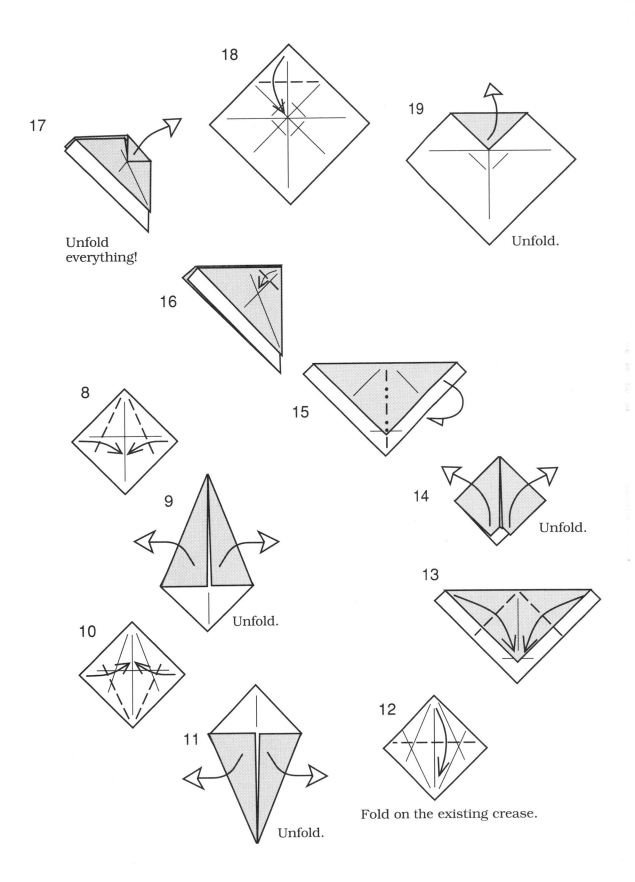

17

Unfold
everything!

18

19

Unfold.

16

15

8

9

Unfold.

14

Unfold.

13

10

11

Unfold.

12

Fold on the existing crease.

TRICERATOPS

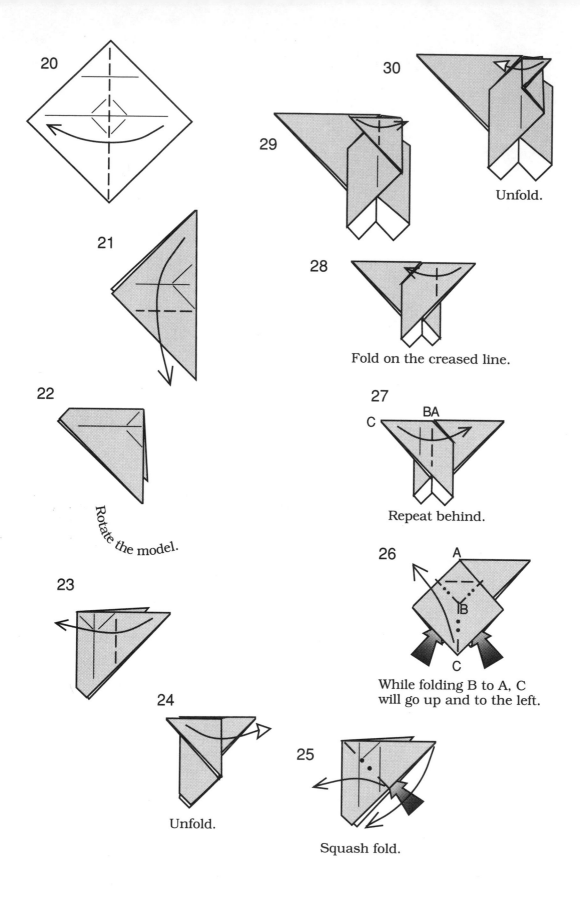

20

21

22

Rotate the model.

23

24

Unfold.

25

Squash fold.

26

A

B

C

While folding B to A, C
will go up and to the left.

27

C   BA

Repeat behind.

28

Fold on the creased line.

29

30

Unfold.

31

32

Unfold.

33

Unfold.

34

Squash fold.

35

Fold B to A while folding
C up and to the right.

39

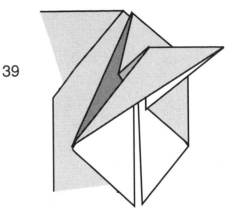

An intermediate step, showing
the formation of the sink fold.

38

Sink.

37

Unfold.

36

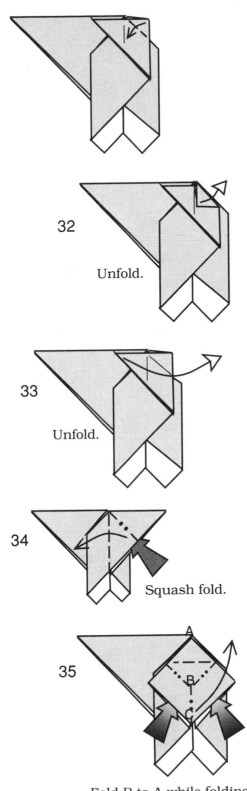

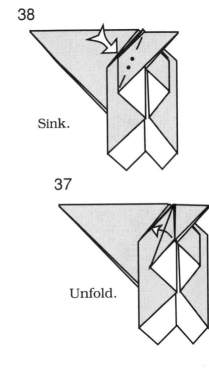

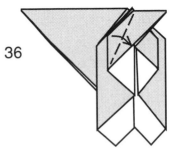

40

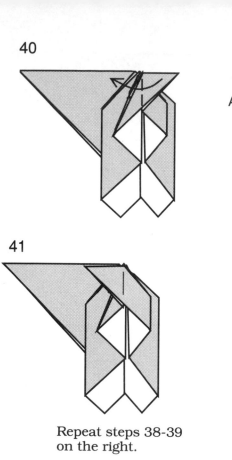

41

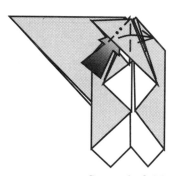

Repeat steps 38-39 on the right.

42

Squash fold.

43

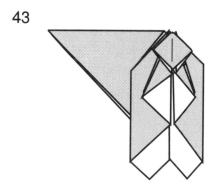

47

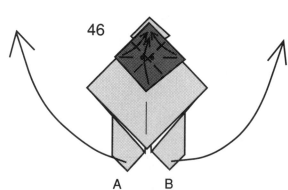

A   B

46

A   B

Make a Preliminary Fold with the darker grey region while folding A and B up.

45

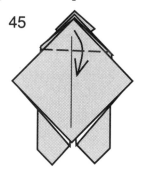

44

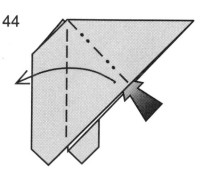

Squash fold.

PREHISTORIC ORIGAMI

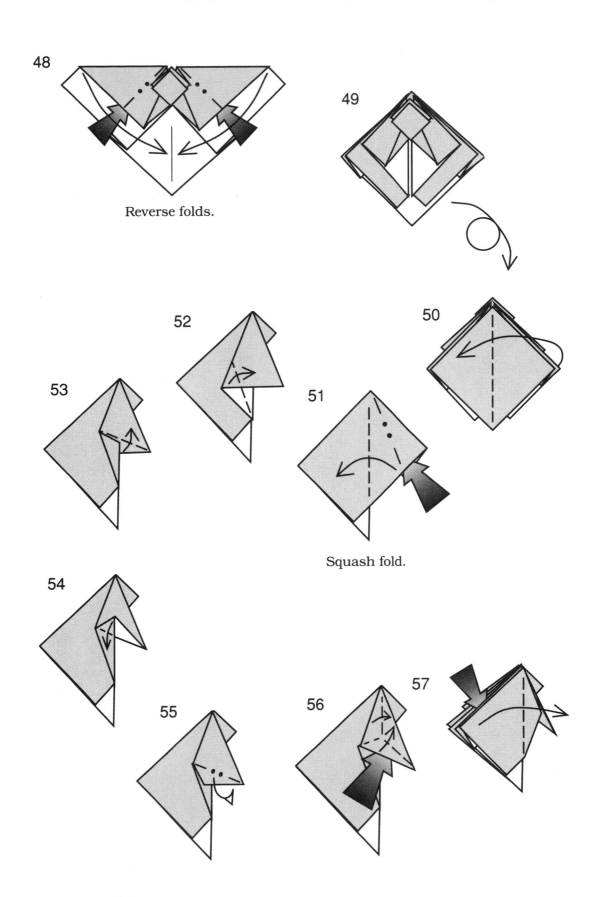

48

Reverse folds.

49

50

51

Squash fold.

52

53

54

55

56

57

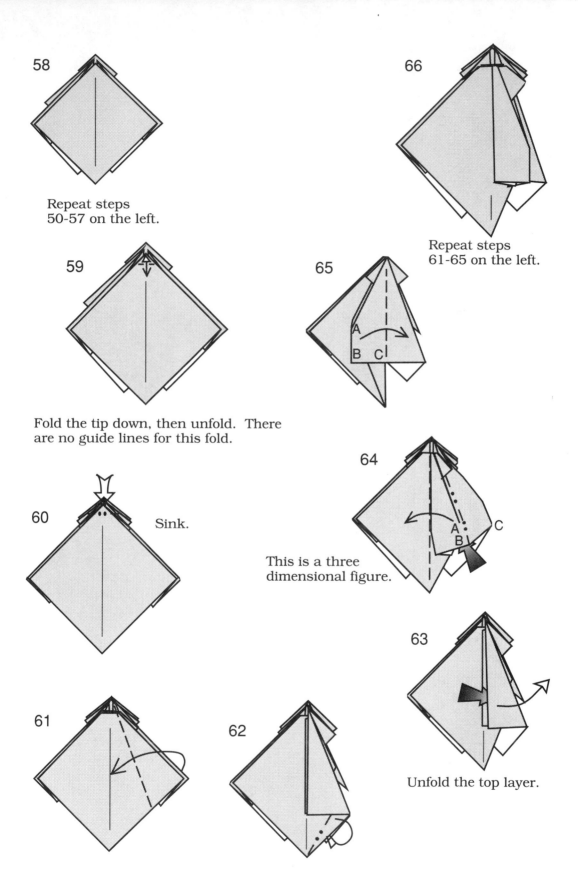

58

Repeat steps
50-57 on the left.

59

Fold the tip down, then unfold. There
are no guide lines for this fold.

60

Sink.

61

62

63

Unfold the top layer.

64

This is a three
dimensional figure.

65

66

Repeat steps
61-65 on the left.

PREHISTORIC ORIGAMI

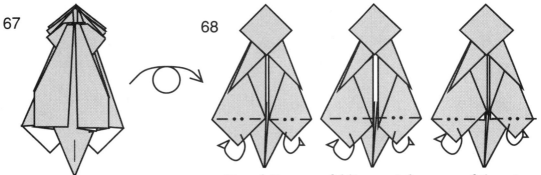

Hopefully, your folding matches one of these! They are all fine, and differ because of the estimated fold in step 6. Be sure that the two mountain folds lie on the same straight line.

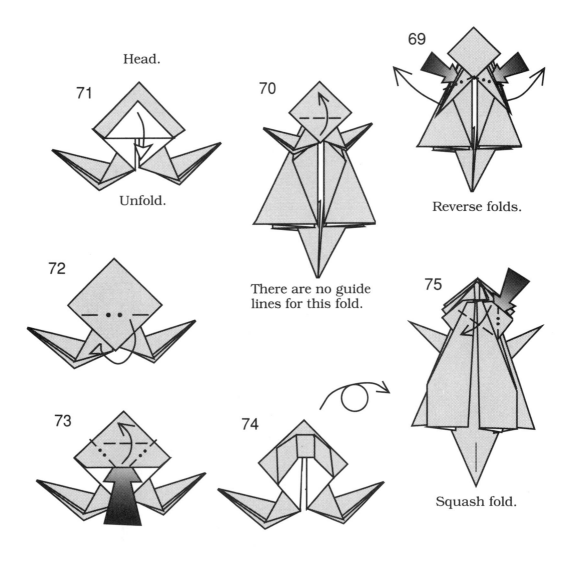

67

68

Head.

71

Unfold.

70

There are no guide lines for this fold.

69

Reverse folds.

72

75

73

74

Squash fold.

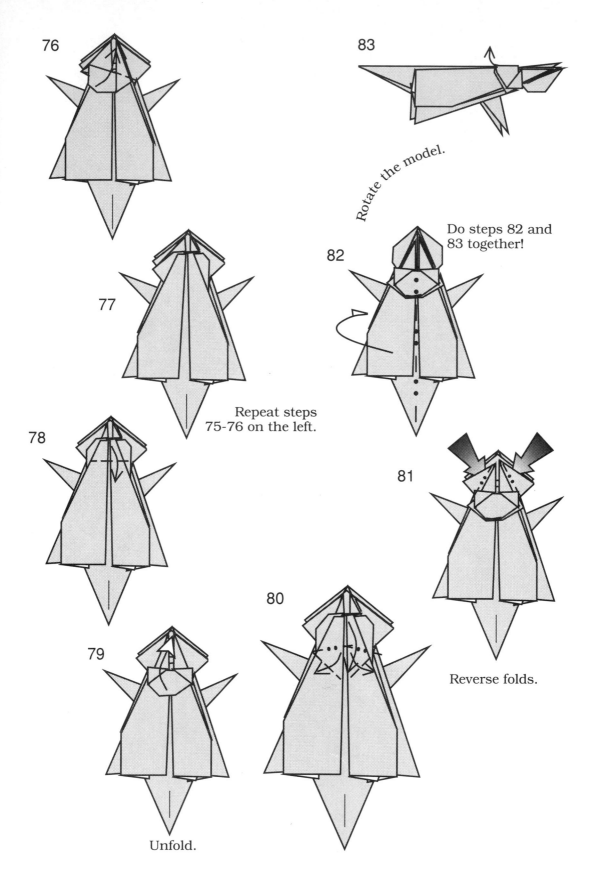

76

83

Rotate the model.

82

Do steps 82 and 83 together!

77

Repeat steps 75-76 on the left.

78

81

80

79

Reverse folds.

Unfold.

PREHISTORIC ORIGAMI

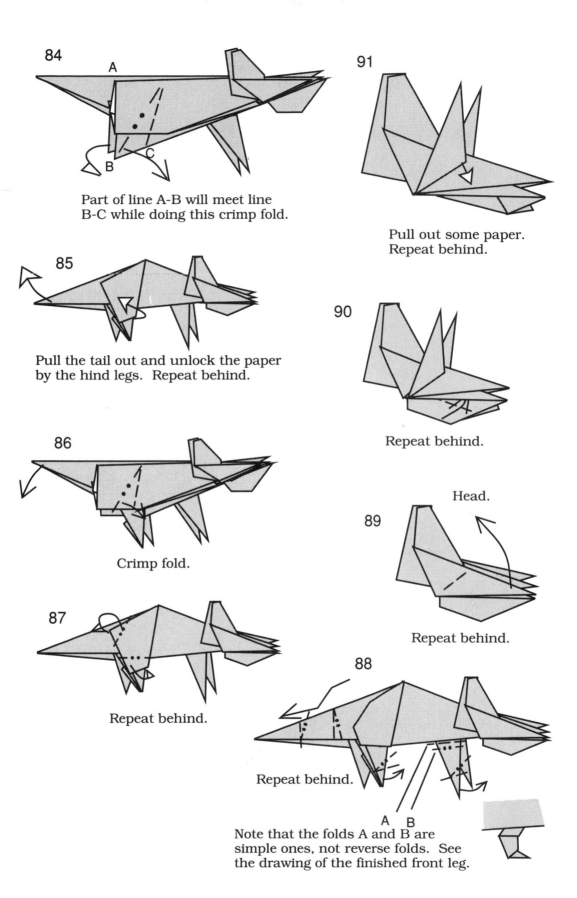

84

A

B C

Part of line A-B will meet line
B-C while doing this crimp fold.

85

Pull the tail out and unlock the paper
by the hind legs. Repeat behind.

86

Crimp fold.

87

Repeat behind.

88

Repeat behind.

A   B

Note that the folds A and B are
simple ones, not reverse folds. See
the drawing of the finished front leg.

91

Pull out some paper.
Repeat behind.

90

Repeat behind.

89

Head.

Repeat behind.

TRICERATOPS

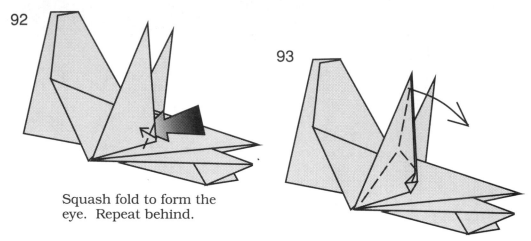

92 Squash fold to form the eye. Repeat behind.

93 Rabbit ear, repeat behind.

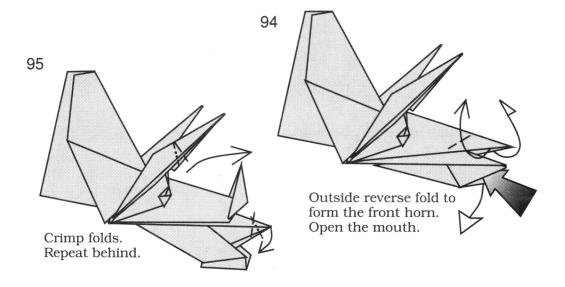

94 Outside reverse fold to form the front horn. Open the mouth.

95 Crimp folds. Repeat behind.

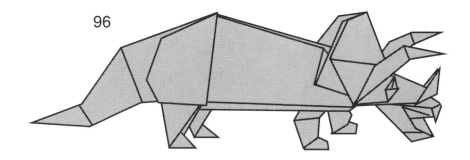

96

Triceratops

Stegosaurus

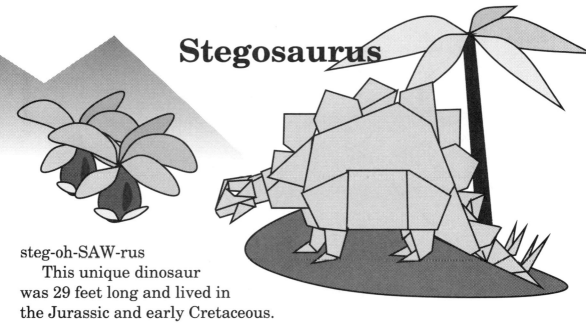

steg-oh-SAW-rus

    This unique dinosaur
was 29 feet long and lived in
the Jurassic and early Cretaceous.
The plates on its back were to regulate its body heat. It had two
walnut size brains. One brain was in its head and the other was at
the base of its tail. This "roof lizard" was found in the western U.S.
and ate plants.

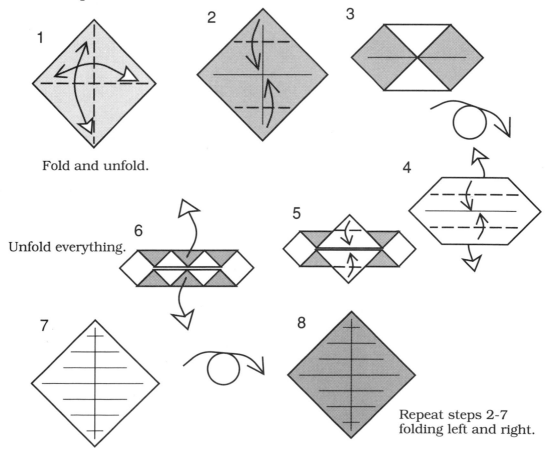

1

Fold and unfold.

2

3

4

5

6

Unfold everything.

7

8

Repeat steps 2-7
folding left and right.

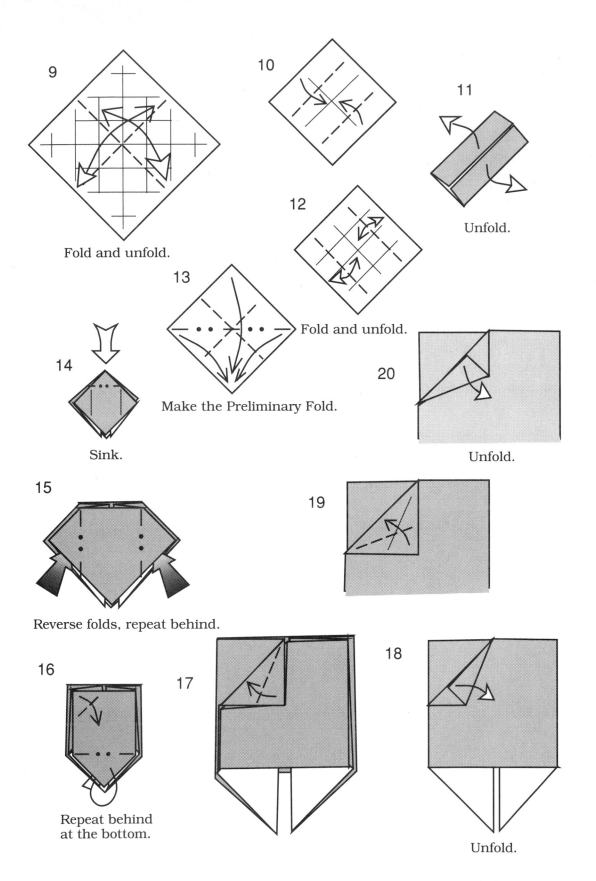

9

Fold and unfold.

10

11

Unfold.

12

Fold and unfold.

13

Make the Preliminary Fold.

14

Sink.

15

Reverse folds, repeat behind.

16

Repeat behind
at the bottom.

17

18

Unfold.

19

20

Unfold.

21

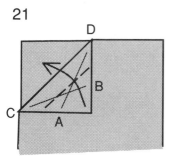

Fold up so that points A and B lie on the line C-D.

22

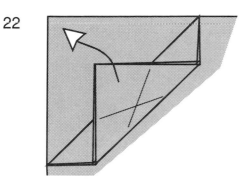

Unfold.

23

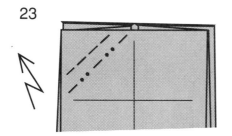

Sink in and out.

24

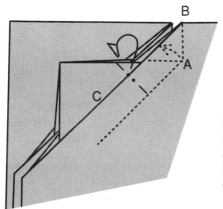

27

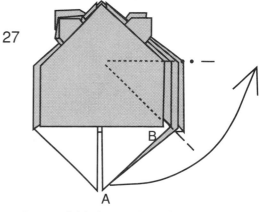

Crimp fold the middle flap.

26

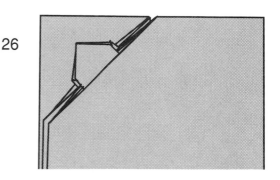

Repeat steps 16 to 25 three times; on the right and back.

25

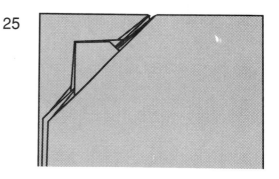

Repeat step 24 three times.

This is a crazy step! The goal is to shape the plate as shown by the mountain line but more folds take place which are hidden. Corner A (which is hidden) will be folded up to the line B-C.

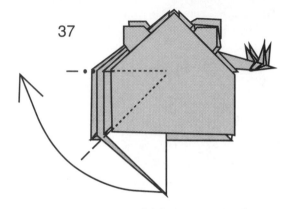

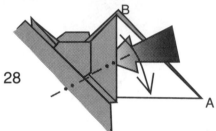

28

Reverse fold, repeat behind.

37

Crimp fold the middle flap.

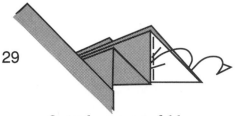

29

Outside reverse fold.

36

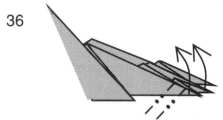

There are five points. The middle one will be the tail - reverse fold the others to form the four spikes. The diagram shows two arrows for the two spikes in front, repeat behind to form the other two.

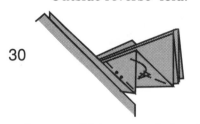

30

Reverse fold, repeat behind.

35

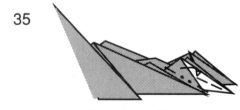

Reverse fold, repeat three times.

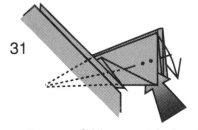

31

Reverse fold, repeat behind.

34

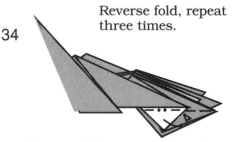

Reverse fold, repeat three times.

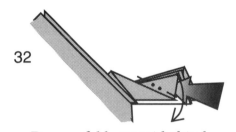

32

Reverse fold, repeat behind.

33

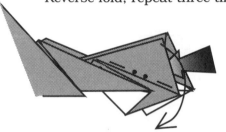

Reverse fold, repeat behind.

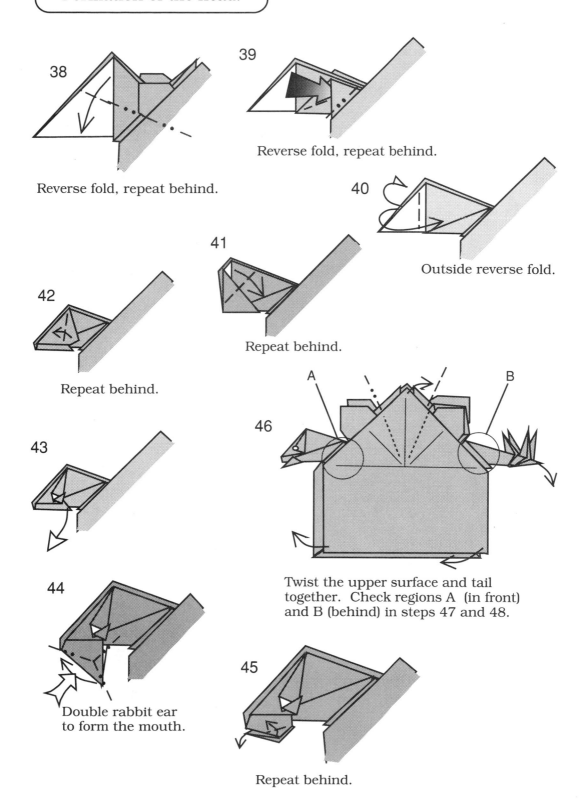

Formation of the head.

38 Reverse fold, repeat behind.

39 Reverse fold, repeat behind.

40 Outside reverse fold.

41 Repeat behind.

42 Repeat behind.

43

44 Double rabbit ear to form the mouth.

45 Repeat behind.

46 Twist the upper surface and tail together. Check regions A (in front) and B (behind) in steps 47 and 48.

A   B

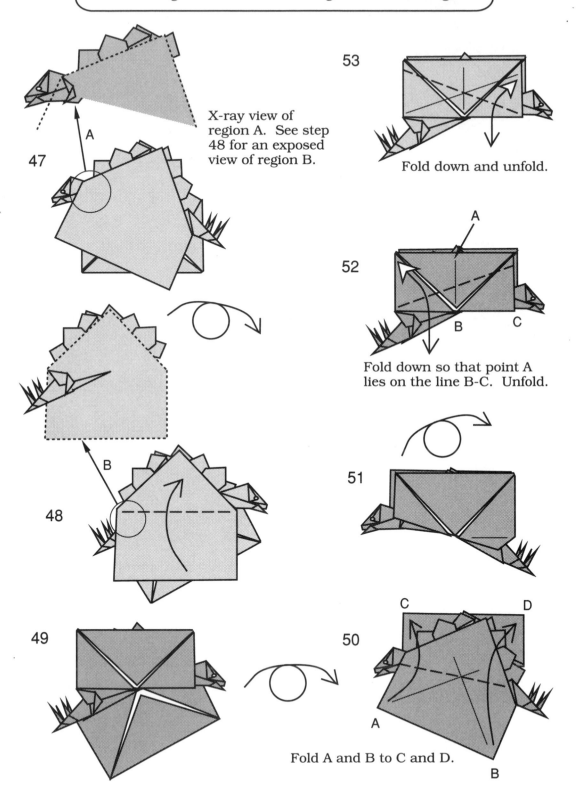

Since the folding is no longer symmetrical, be sure to orient your model according to the drawings!

47

X-ray view of region A. See step 48 for an exposed view of region B.

48

49

50

Fold A and B to C and D.

51

52

Fold down so that point A lies on the line B-C. Unfold.

53

Fold down and unfold.

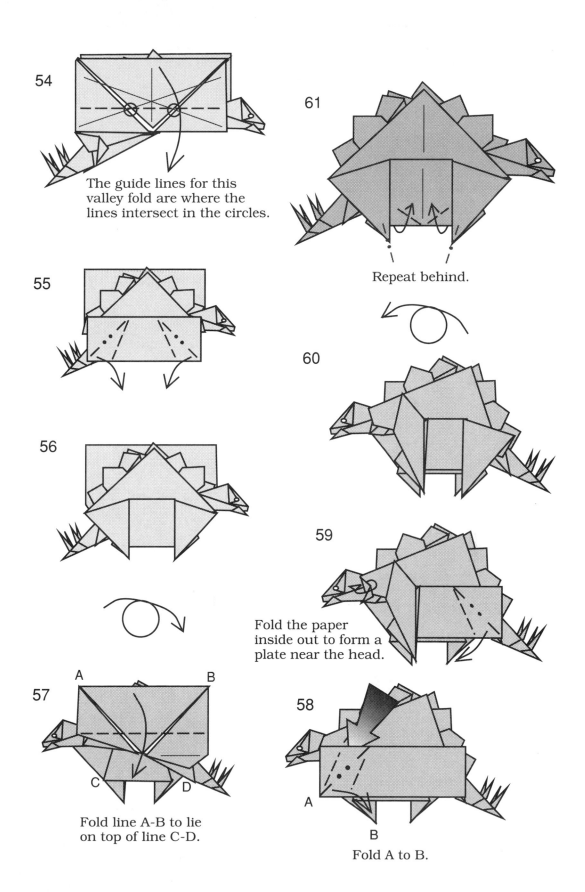

54

The guide lines for this valley fold are where the lines intersect in the circles.

55

56

57

A   B

C   D

Fold line A-B to lie on top of line C-D.

61

Repeat behind.

60

59

Fold the paper inside out to form a plate near the head.

58

A

B

Fold A to B.

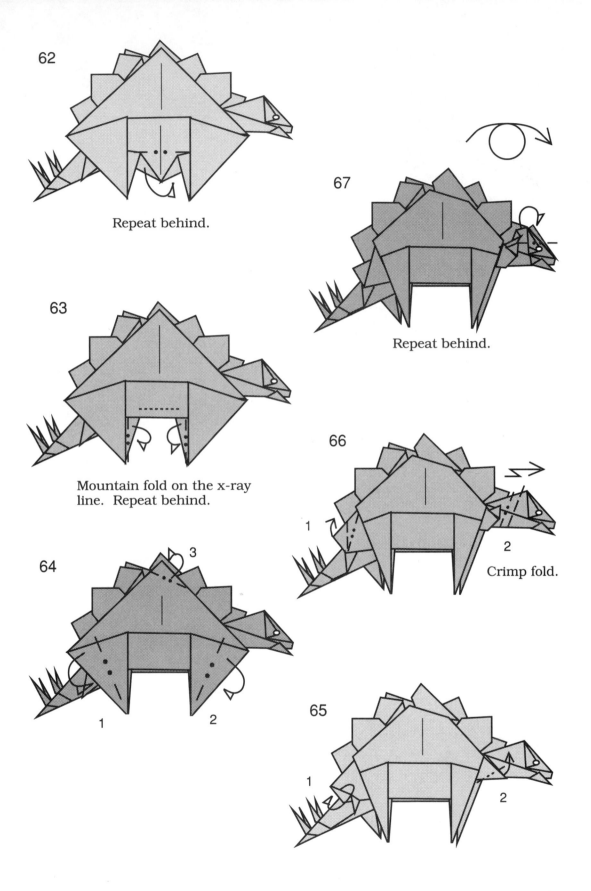

62

Repeat behind.

63

Mountain fold on the x-ray
line. Repeat behind.

64

1   2

67

Repeat behind.

66

1

2

Crimp fold.

65

1

2

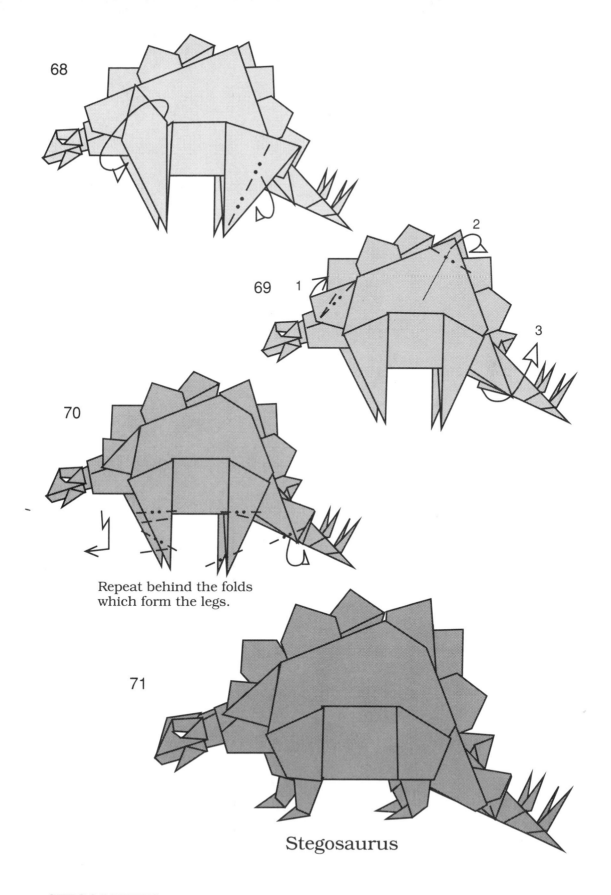

68

69 1 2 3

70

Repeat behind the folds
which form the legs.

71

Stegosaurus